# THE SUPERWOMAN ENTREPRENEUR

## How to Turn Your Breakdowns into Breakthroughs to Live a Life of Peace, Play, & Prosperity

Maribel Jimenez

# DEDICATION

To the biggest supporters in my life who watched me go on this path and transform into the woman I am today—my mom, Eloisa, and my dad, Eleazar; my siblings Marisa and Gilbert; my kids, Ricky, Xavier, Nicole, Alyssa; and my husband, Paul—thank you for your love, guidance and always believing in me.

To all the women out there who want to design a business and life of Peace, Play, & Prosperity: there is no perfect time so choose to breakthrough any challenges and tap into the SUPERwoman in you. It's my mission to help you in any way to create the life you dream of. And together with all the other women entrepreneurs featured in this book, we want to share our journeys, practices, steps and guidance with you to go after what you desire to create.

You Got This!

# CONTENTS

# ACKNOWLEDGMENTS

This book was a labor of love and I could not have done it without the support and contribution of all the amazing Superwoman Entrepreneur Co-Authors who are featured in this book. They joined me in having the courage to share some deep and personal breakthroughs that for some, was a first time to publicly share. Thank you for inspiring me every step of the way and believing in me and this book to help others on their journeys. I'm forever grateful.

Thank you to my amazing book support team: Ginger Johnson, Carol Ann DeSimine, Serena Trebizo, Kim Eldredge, Holly Doherty, and Melissa Forte, for helping to bring this book forward in the best way. You all gave your book expertise, support, countless hours, and wisdom all the way to the finish line. With you behind me, I knew we'd create something great.

I thank my family for all the love and encouragement. My mom and dad, who instilled the desire to go after my dreams and were always there when I needed them. My sister, Marisa, who has the biggest heart, inspires me and is an amazing example of a SUPERwoman. My brother, Gilbert, who always showed so much strength and was never afraid to tell me the straight up truth when I was going off course. My husband, Paul, who's been by my side, holding my hand and supporting me the many times I needed space to work on this book.

And to my online community of Superwoman Entrepreneurs, you inspire me each day to move past my fears and keep showing up because it is changing lives for the better. Thank you for being open to the healing and practices to make your own powerful impact in the world. I hope this book supports you in that journey.

For every woman who heals herself helps heal all the women who came before her, and all those who come after her.

~ Christiane Northrup

# THE SUPERWOMAN
# ENTREPRENEUR

She has big dreams and willing to go after them.

She understands that true power comes from within and by honoring who she is.

She has the courage to speak her truth.

She embraces her own uniqueness and loves and honors herself.

She knows how to take good care of herself and overflows to others.

She loves herself and overflows with love for others.

She respects herself and has no need to prove anything.

She honors her intuition and higher power.

She gives herself permission to have fun, play and laugh every day.

She looks for the blessings in disguise and encourages her own growth.

She is grateful for the gifts she has and shares them.

She honors the flow of giving and receiving.

She opens her heart to heal and help others heal past or current wounds.

She understands her life is an expression of what's inside and manifests her desires.

She's gentle with herself and shows it in every area of life.

*Nothing can dim the light that shines from within.*

~ Maya Angelou

# THE SUPERWOMAN
# ENTREPRENEUR PATHWAY

The Superwoman Entrepreneur™ Pathway is a way of life—not a destination. Each step you take, you will deepen your transformation. These seven core areas have totally transformed my life. I want to highlight each one and give you some action steps as you begin your own journey.

There are several layers underneath each area that create more shifts. Those layers are exactly why I designed the Superwoman Entrepreneur™ Retreat to be able to experience the elements. I also host the Superwoman Entrepreneur Podcast to share concepts from each area, along with real life stories from my experiences and other women—such as those featured in this book!

These are all steps that can be taken to begin making positive shifts that align with your best self in the Superwoman Entrepreneur Pathway. It's a practice and way of living that gets nurtured each day.

## 1. Your Superwoman Vision

Vision is defined as, "the ability to think about or plan the future with imagination or wisdom".

I define your Superwoman Vision as the BIG vision you have. This vision might scare you, but it's truly for you and not to prove anything to anyone else.

Your Superwoman Vision may feel too big, or even too simple. As an overachiever, what I wanted was simplicity. And having a Superwoman Vision that was all about ease and flow felt too big and too simple—and it was exactly what I wanted.

Your Superwoman Vision may not even feel possible to you. It is not the goal for you to figure out how to accomplish your Superwoman vision; it's your goal to define it and connect with it.

Creating your Superwoman Vision is the first step towards having what you desire. In order to have your desires come to fruition, you must connect with what you want, and what success looks like for you.

Do you have a secret desire or dream that you want to "someday" have? What does that look like for you? Give yourself an opportunity to connect with it.

## Action Step:

**Create your own Superwoman Vision of what a successful life looks like for you.** Sit down, close your eyes, and take three deep breaths. See in your mind's eye what a day in the life of your dreams looks like for you. Are there key elements that stand out that you desire?

For me, it was the desire for Peace, Play, and Prosperity every day. Those were key in my definition of success. Then I went deeper with the experience of a day where I could see and feel Peace, Play, and Prosperity. What was I doing? Who was there with me?

Your turn. I invite you to journal about your Superwoman Vision. I promise, it gets clearer and clearer over time as you begin to focus on what you want and not on what you don't want.

## 2. Your Superwoman Inner Feminine

Everyone has masculine and feminine energy. When the balance of those energies is misaligned, life and business feel harder. As a woman, you were designed with more feminine energy—but you still have masculine energy.

The masculine energy is about doing and the feminine energy is about being. You need both to feel in alignment.

Early in my journey, I realized I had spent so many years focused on my masculine side of doing more, and working my way up the ladder in management, that I didn't even know how to access that feminine side. Sound familiar?

When I began this work on myself, I hired a mentor to understand how to tap into my feminine energy. My mentor invited me to access this powerful energy. Once I did life began to feel joyful and I felt so much more ease. I didn't have to try so hard anymore, I felt energized and supported. I practiced "receiving", a feminine energy and felt fulfilled and balanced.

I wasn't just giving (and giving, and giving) all the time, until there was nothing left to give.

## Action Steps:

**Practice receiving by showing self-love.** There are many ways to practice self-love, here are a few of my favorites. Pick any of them that resonate with you and I invite you to do the one that feels the hardest. You will experience the biggest shift by doing the actions that feel hard.

**Look in the mirror and give yourself a compliment.** What's one thing you love about yourself? Want a bigger challenge? Try doing this naked in front of the mirror.

**Pay yourself first.** Put at least 10% of your income aside for play and then use it to treat yourself to something special without apology or justification. (It doesn't always have to cost money either!)

**Receive a compliment without explaining yourself or putting yourself down.** I used to always feel the need to say something back versus just saying "Thank you!" and fully receiving the compliment.

**Take care of your inner child.** Close your eyes and see yourself at five years old. Then ask your inner child, "What do you need today? What feels fun? What feels like play for you today? Is there anything you need today to feel loved?"

You may feel like taking a nap, a walk, sitting quietly to enjoy your favorite drink, or going out to have some girl time. This is about doing what feels like play to you. The more you play, the more fun your life becomes.

**Be your own raving fan with your self-talk.** Your self-talk is either building you up or bringing you down. Pay attention to what you are saying and make an effort to catch yourself if it isn't building you up. Learn to pivot in the moment with a positive self-talk statement. The goal is to be your own biggest supporter.

## 3. Develop Superwoman Relationships

I've learned that the people in our lives are our teachers. One of the mistakes I used to make was thinking that I should avoid any conflict with others. I believe the people that show up in our lives always have a purpose.

If you're relationships aren't impacting you in a good way, there may be a blessing in disguise to support you. Whether it's for your learning or theirs, or both, it's in the challenge that the growth happens.

## Action Step:

**Practice seeing the gift in everyone who is in your life.** It's easy to find fault in someone, if you look for it, since nobody is perfect. When you focus on the gift in another person, you will immediately change your experience.

## 4. Superwoman Wellness

Self-care, self-love, and how you treat yourself have an impact on your life. When you are taken care of, you love to give from a place of overflow. So, ask yourself how you're taking care of yourself. And then be honest about where you're treating yourself well and where you're not! Examples might be: Do you give yourself time off or are you working all the time? Do you pay yourself first or do you live on the financial scraps?

## Action Steps:

**Pick one or more actions below to nurture your body.** I invite you start with the area that you feel needs the most attention. Be gentle with yourself and keep taking steps. Here are the top five things I do each day to feel my best:

1. **Eat things that feed my body.** This isn't about perfection, but rather ensuring I'm paying attention to how I'm supporting my body with the fuel that it needs to feel energized and heal itself. The simplest tip I've learned is to focus on incorporating foods that are in their most natural form from the earth. The more ingredients added to food, the less nutrition, if any, is left.

2. **Hydrate.** The easy tip is to only drink water instead of sugary drinks. Again, it's not about being perfect, but instead adding water to hydrate. I love my morning cup of coffee and because I understand that caffeine dehydrates, I incorporate 8-10 glasses of water throughout the day.

3. **Movement.** When I move, I get the benefits of serotonin (the feel-good chemical). I enjoy yoga, walking, running, being active with my kids. I even make it a point to go up and down the stairs as often as I can because I sit at my computer a lot.

4. **Shot of Braggs® apple cider vinegar every day.** There are many books on the benefits of having 1-2 tablespoons of apple cider vinegar each day so I will just share the top five reasons I take it: it purifies your blood, reduces belly fat, kills many types of bacteria, aids in digestion, and has many anti-aging properties.

5. **Rest.** Listen to my body. When I feel tired, my body is talking to me, so I take a break with a power nap. I'm also sure to get the amount of sleep I need every night to recharge and heal my body. To feel my best, that means a full eight hours of sleep.

## 5. Superwoman Healing

I believe healing practices are important in life. Just like exercise, you don't just go the gym once and think, "I'm done with exercise for the rest of my life." Most people think, "If I've reached my ideal weight, I don't need to exercise anymore!" It's the exercise that got you there so you would continue to do it.

That's what I believe about healing. It's a life-long practice. There are so many different modalities of healing that support you in thriving.

## Action Step:

Incorporate a form of healing. This could be as simple as laughing, crying, journaling, rest, and many special deeper healing modalities that release trauma. These forms of healing all release energy built up inside. With any energy you feel strongly, it needs to be released in some way. Energy can't be destroyed; it just builds up unless you release it.

## 6. Your Superwoman Leap

Your Superwoman Leap is stretching yourself and expanding into your full potential. In order to expand, you must push past your comfort zone and be willing to be uncomfortable knowing that's where the growth happens. In challenging yourself to face your fears, you grow in confidence that you can achieve anything you set your mind to.

## Action Step:

Do the thing that scares you most each day. Ask yourself, "What am I most afraid of doing right now?" Whatever that thing is, if you know it will provide the growth you are looking for, then take the next step towards it.

My biggest fear was public speaking. To overcome it, I hired a mentor who taught me how to create my presentations effectively. Then, I went out to get my first speaking engagement before I could shrink back into my fear. I challenged myself to do it despite the huge fear (and how much sleep I was losing over it). I knew that speaking was exactly what would move me forward in sharing my mission. Now I speak every week because changing lives is important enough to me that I'm willing to feel the fear and do it anyway.

## 7. Your Superwoman Flow

This is about inviting the flow every day. I call it flow when everything seems to be working out, on time and perfectly.

Have you experienced being in the flow? Doesn't it feel like everything is working out in your favor? That's because it is!

## Action Steps:

**Shift your perspective to trust that everything is working *for* you.** What if you shifted your perspective to "Trusting that the Universe or God is conspiring on your behalf"?

If you've studied the law of attraction, you know that like attracts like. What you send out, you receive, at a vibrational level. I invite you to play with this concept. Pay attention to your thoughts and see where you can shift perspective and trust that everything is working out in your favor. Everything is happening *for you* not *to you*.

**Clear clutter everywhere.** Do you have an organized and clean workspace, or are there stacks of papers everywhere? Clutter is draining. You use energy when you look at it and think about what you have to get done, or how you can't wait until you have time to put it all away. Then, there's the energy you use when you are looking for something and there are papers or folders everywhere – it can be exhausting.

**Set intentions in all areas.** Setting an intention allows you to live intentionally versus being at the effect of it. Without consciously setting an intention, you are still sending a signal with the thoughts and feelings you have.

It's the difference between waking up and telling yourself you feel tired. Then yes, you will feel that state of tiredness because you will automatically feel it and think matching thoughts like "I wish I could sleep more" or "I can't think straight I'm so tired" or "I feel foggy", etc.

Yet if you wake up and tell yourself you are excited for what today will bring and set an intention to feel energized, you'll notice the match to that intention. This becomes thoughts like, "I feel great, it's going to be a great day" and "I'm excited for what today will bring", etc.

Do you see how quickly you can change your state?

**Whatever you desire in your heart, write it out with clarity.** Don't worry about what it will take to make it real; just go directly to the end result of what you want to experience.

Superwoman Entrepreneur Pathway has been my mission for the last eight years when I began my own deep transformation to see how good life could be.

And I'm still on that journey of living life each day with Peace, Play, and Prosperity. I invite you to go on it with me and find the "gold" in the many breakthrough stories shared.

Let the journey begin,

*Maribel*

The future belongs to those who believe in the beauty of their dreams.

~ Eleanor Roosevelt

# THE BIRTH OF MY SUPERWOMAN ENTREPRENEUR MISSION

I am peaceful, playful and prosperous every day.

*Maribel Jimenez*

My life was filled with breakdowns. And before I knew any better, I let my heart harden with each one of them. I learned to shove my feelings down deep and pretend like they weren't there. Life felt normal to me that way.

My uncle molested me when I was eight years old. I was raped at thirteen years old, robbed of my virginity and filled with shame and blame. At nineteen years old, I was beaten and raped again and this time I thought I was going to die that night.

I wasn't ready to die. I remember praying to God to live longer, so I could raise my son, who was two years old at the

15

time. Then, that night as a bat was raised to hit me, the abuser suddenly snapped out of his fit of rage and broke down on the floor crying. The nightmare ended. God had given me the miracle I prayed for—another chance.

My feelings disappeared completely. It felt like a movie— as if it didn't actually happen. People told me I needed therapy but I didn't feel anything. I didn't cry or get sad. I just focused on living what I thought was a normal life.

In actuality, I lived on autopilot, doing what I was "supposed to" do—follow the rules, go to school, and work my way up the career ladder so I could live happily ever after.

Within several years, I had what looked like a dream life. I was married with two kids, pregnant with my third child, and living by the beach with a six-figure career. It all looked great from the outside.

But I was exhausted from trying to be good at everything. I was a workaholic, working much harder than necessary in order to achieve my goals. In my quest to have it all, I beat myself up to be better, to do more, and to sacrifice to make ends meet.

Every day was filled with cooking, cleaning, laundry, errands, schoolwork, studying, mom duties, business work, and the never-ending to-do list. I kept going and going, trying to be as perfect as possible—the Superwoman who "did it all" and also looked good doing it.

I didn't ask for help with anything and my huge to-do list was never finished. I continually put my own needs last and could barely keep up.

My limiting beliefs told me, "It takes hard work, so just suck it up. You want to be successful. This is what it looks like. Work now; play later. Your family will thank you later."

But slowly, my heart started to remind me of the secret dream I'd held since I was five years old—to run my own business. I was tired of working myself into the ground for everyone else. It was time to live *my* dream and create what I truly wanted.

I knew that there was no perfect time to start my own business. So took a leap forward and left my fifteen-year career in marketing and business development so I could launch my dream. If I could create success as an employee in marketing, why couldn't I do it for *myself?*

I remember praying in my car that day. It seemed ridiculous to give up the job at which I'd worked so hard to excel. I'd finally I met my goal of making six figures and gained the respect of an almost-all-male management team who thought I was just a pretty face with no brains. That was not easy to do. It took me years.

But despite the fear, I started to feel excited—like a kid who was about to get a new toy.

I felt a peace inside, knowing that God was with me in that moment. It felt safe to do what I had always wanted to do. I knew it was divine timing to make the move, and there was no going back to it.

Then, the *real* journey to find my inner Superwoman began.

All the "fake it until you make it" tactics didn't work anymore. All the masks, defense mechanisms, and lies I told myself were useless.

When I got into alignment with my soul's purpose, I began to experience life differently. I began to *feel* my feelings, to become *present* to what life is all about, and to experience *real* joy.

It's like I could finally *see*. Life looked and felt very different.

It wasn't about hurrying up to achieve and prove myself anymore. Instead, I focused on the journey itself – living each day like it was my last, full-out in my own Superwoman way.

So what did it take to break this new Superwoman in me wide open and connect to my heart – my soul's calling – and to experience the flow?

A *big* breakdown!

This breakdown led to my breakthrough and the birth of my new mission.

I was sleeping when the phone rang in the middle of the night. It was my son's dad, calling from the hospital to tell me that my son had been hospitalized.

I was frozen in that moment, filled with adrenaline, waiting to hear the details. I sat there in shock while he told me that my son had overdosed on pills and was hallucinating.

As tears rolled down my cheeks and my heart ached, my son took the phone and started talking to me. His words didn't make any sense. I listened while he shared bits and pieces about his childhood, like an episode of SpongeBob SquarePants™ that made him laugh.

In that moment, all I wanted to do was hold him and take away the pain he felt. I sat there with my heart broken, blaming myself. How did I miss the signs of him in pain? Why didn't I pay more attention?

I thought about what would have happened if I'd lost my son that night.

All along, I'd worked so hard on my new venture as an entrepreneur to replace my old salary and provide my family with what I thought they needed. I focused so much on creating a successful business that I missed out on things. I thought that if I worked hard in the moment, I could play later.

It pained me to realize that I'd put work above my family's needs. I'd ignored them in the present moment so we could celebrate later. I was there, but I wasn't present.

Being successful definitely wasn't more important than my son, but my actions showed otherwise.

My son didn't need more money or more stuff. He needed his mom to be *present*.

I realized that I didn't want that life anymore if it meant I couldn't see the clues of a problem with my son, and if we wouldn't have the connection necessary for him to talk to me and get support. I didn't want my plate to be so packed that I couldn't spend time with my loved ones regularly.

At the end of the day, I don't want to be remembered by my family as someone who got stuff done and always made sure the bills were paid. I want to be remembered for having a beautiful connection with my family, making wonderful memories and being present to the gift of having them in my life.

That was my *big* wakeup call!

I cried for the first time in a really long time. I prayed that God would show me what it would take for me to live a life where I felt peaceful, playful, and prosperous every day.

I wanted peace, knowing that I was a good mom and wife, taking care of the most important things and not just doing everything I could "on the list".

I wanted a life where I honored the gifts God has given me. I wanted to feel the peace in my heart that I was in alignment with my soul's purpose, trusting that God had a better plan for me than I did, and knowing that all I had to do was listen and take action.

I wanted to play again and have fun in life, not having to choose between success and fun. At that time in my life, I was so numb. Nothing was fun. I was resentful and irritable. My cup was empty, and I was running on fumes.

I missed that playful girl inside of me who loved to laugh, who loved to be with people and have fun with her family. It was time to bring her back.

I realized that I could have fun each day, starting right then. I needed to do what I loved and be present with the special gifts life presented to me each day. And I needed to be myself again. It was time to let go of all the beliefs and judgments I held about myself that didn't serve me.

And the third element I craved was prosperity. I was so tired of worrying about bills and other obligations. I justified the way I put everything else aside to work as doing my part to earn the money we needed to survive, but it all came from a scarcity mindset.

So I prayed for that worry to stop and to have more than enough money to live the life we desired. I was ready to do it God's way and to trust that I would be guided on this new path. I had already tried it my way and did not find the peace, playfulness, and prosperity that I craved.

After my prayer, I felt peace again and committed to a new way of life. For the next thirty days, I paused everywhere in my life. I knew I couldn't keep doing the same things and expect a different result - that's the definition of insanity.

I immersed myself in prayer, quiet time, and healing modalities. I connected with my new vision and my inner feminine. I focused on taking care of myself and everything that was important to me – especially relationships and family.

I discovered the New Superwoman Entrepreneur way, focused on practices to restore my feminine power, honor my gifts, and tap into what makes me unique. It meant falling in love with myself instead of criticizing or beating myself up.

It was a full-life transformation – a new me. I was filled with love, light, and an overflowing desire to help others. I was happy from the inside and I didn't have to fake it anymore.

It was freeing! No more "shoulds". No more living by other people's rules or beliefs, and no more judging my every move.

I designed my whole life differently. And I continue to nurture this way of life in a community, surrounding myself with other women who live this way.

My son went on this journey with me, and I'm grateful for the beautiful relationship we share today. He has grown using the elements of the Superwoman I share in this book. (Yes, it works for men, too. But I focus on my journey as a woman.)

I am passionate about sharing with other women what is possible when they allow themselves to tap into what makes them *super*.

When you do what you are here on earth to do, life is filled with flow.

When you tap into who you are—your unique strengths and the gifts you have—and allow yourself to have what your heart desires, life is peaceful, playful, and prosperous. There's nothing you can't do.

The Superwoman inside of you wants to spread her wings and thrive!

You deserve to have all your heart's desires come to fruition. You have everything inside to make it happen. You are powerful. You have gifts that no one else has. You are perfect just as you were created.

You may be in pain right now. Maybe you're in the middle of a breakthrough at this moment, and ready to make some changes to get on a new path.

Your breakdowns and challenges are not obstacles to stop you; they are there to guide you, to stretch you, and to help you align with your true desires.

Every breakdown moves you forward in a powerful way. If you look for it, each one has a "blessing in disguise" that opens the door to a new way of doing things, a new strength you didn't realize you had, or a new opportunity to pursue. Breakdowns generate the shifts necessary to create what you want in your life.

My prayer is that you get clarity on where your breakdowns are leading you. What lesson can you learn? What changes do you crave? What do you want to stop doing?

Connect with the vision of your life that you desire.

In this book, I share the eight core areas that shifted to align with the Superwoman Entrepreneur way of life.

You will see many examples of these shifts in the breakthrough stories from other Superwomen Entrepreneurs, along with a collection of tools, practices, and advice to help you on your own journey.

I don't have all the answers. I believe in coming together with a shared purpose so we can all win. That's why I brought together many different women to share with you.

It is no accident that you are reading this book right now, at this divinely perfect time, to receive exactly the practices, words, and advice that you need. I invite you to embrace what resonates and leave the rest. There is no "one way for all".

It's my intention that you get the wisdom that is perfect for you, and that it moves you forward in designing the life your heart desires.

Connect with the vision of your life that you desire.

~ Maribel Jimenez

# STAYING ALIGNED WITH
# MY BELIEFS
## I am following my heart.

*Chen Yen*

## My Superwoman Breakthrough

I started out as a pharmacist on Native American reservations. At first, I was very excited about traveling to different reservations, meeting various cultures and tribes, and having adventures. But after a while, I started feeling very dissatisfied going to work every day.

I remember handing this woman her Prozac® medication, and feeling angry—not at her, but at what our healthcare system had to offer her. I felt as if I was endorsing these medications, even though I didn't believe that they were the best option.

I grew up in a family that believed in more holistic choices. As a child, when I got sick, my mom might open up the cabinet and pull out some Chinese herbal therapy. That was the extent of it.

Today, I always hear about doctors giving people ten or twenty different medications as if they are bags of candy. I saw little kids come in, get immunization shots, and leave with a cocktail of medications.

I felt like I had to get out of there, even though I didn't know what I wanted to do instead.

I noticed pharmacists around me who were counting down towards retirement from their government jobs. I thought, "That doesn't feel like a way to live: you have fifteen years and two days left." I wondered if I could help them get into jobs they enjoyed more.

So fast forward five years. I had started a successful pharmacist recruiting business, growing it to seven figures in less than five years. I used to think that if I just made more money, then I could do what I really cared about outside of work. But it didn't happen that way for me.

I did a lot of soul searching, and I realized that I needed to stop pretending. Because I was still felt like I was selling my soul for people to be on drugs when I'm actually extremely holistic. For example, I don't own a cell phone, and I still don't ever see myself owning one.

I thought about how our healthcare system could actually be more integrated. I believe won't be the insurance companies that do it. It won't be the drug companies or the government changing things.

Change will come from people who offer options outside of the conventional medical system—holistic options that can be very beneficial. But holistic practitioners often run into two big issues. First, they have so much to offer, but people don't even know that type of help exists. Second, they went to school to help people, but not necessarily run a business. They often struggle with that side of things.

I decided to help holistic health practitioners—acupuncturists, chiropractors, naturopathic doctors, and functional medicine practitioners—to grow their businesses in a way that fills up their schedule so they can focus on helping people instead of worrying about where to find people to help.

I help holistic practitioners who are already busy with patients, but there's only so much time in the day and only one of them to go around. They want to make a bigger impact without always having to be there. So I help them scale to multi-six and seven figures and in a way that's comfortable for them as an introvert.

## My Tools & Rituals to Stay in the Flow

The journey of finding my true passion was never a straight line. It was a constant process of realizing that I didn't feel good about my current work and asking myself what I wanted. When I went in that direction, I felt excited and realized, "Wow, this is so cool!"

As for peacefulness and balance, meditation has been very powerful for me. I also had transformative experiences within Indian enlightenment master Parma Ham. Those extremely powerful energy initiations reset my body at the core.

I feel like I'm at peace all the time, so I don't really feel like there's anything I need to do, except to just be.

For playfulness, I love dancing ballet. I actually wanted to be a ballerina when I was little. My parents told me I couldn't make any money doing that. So I danced a little bit when I was younger, but then I stopped. I picked it back up, then stopped for a while again. Recently, I started dancing a few days a week. It's brought me so much joy.

I was accepted at the Peabody Conservatory of Music and had planned to become a professional violinist. After a series of events, such as my dad telling me not to go, I ended up going to pharmacy school instead.

I still enjoy music. However, as an adult, I didn't play for a long time. One day I went to ballet class, and an amazing Russian pianist accompanied us. Her music made me dance better because it was so beautiful. After class, I asked her if she ever played with a violinist. As we talked further, she asked,

"Do you want to play with me at a performance? I'm having one next weekend."

So then we practiced. She's incredible—a beautifully talented pianist who has thousands of pieces memorized. It's such a blessing to be able to play with her.

Before the concert, she asked me to send her my bio. I thought to myself, "What bio?" I decided to pull something together quickly.

As I thought about what to write, I looked up a place in Austria where I once played. I discovered that they were playing an amazing repertoire of music. Now, I'm going to Austria to play with them!

So for me, peacefulness and play is about seeing what inspires me in that moment and then following that hunch. That process continues to bring more into peacefulness and play into my life.

## My Purpose Is

We help acupuncturists, chiropractors, naturopathic doctors and functional medicine practitioners who love what they're doing, but don't like the marketing side of things. They wish that they could just focus on seeing their patients and helping more people. We use different systems, depending on the stage of their practice, to help them grow in a way that feels comfortable for them, especially as an introvert.

A lot of approaches out there are geared towards extroverts. But 30-50% of people are actually introverts. Standard advice like, "put yourself out there" or "go out and network" feels exhausting for introverts. They need a different approach. When our clients work with us through our Introverted Visionaries, six- and seven-figure systems, they grow their businesses with ease and flow. They no longer try to force themselves to do things that aren't right for them.

Speaking is a great way for introverts to reach more people at once without having to always put themselves "out there".

Our Six-Figure Speaking System for Introverts teaches them how to do that.

Our clients want to grow to multiple-six and seven figures. But as they get busier, they face some unique challenges. They often feel overwhelmed. They believe that they can't leave their practice without negatively impacting their patients' care. If they take a vacation, they might not make the money they need. And sometimes, the more money they make in the practice, the less they actually keep.

We help them put systems in place that allow the practices to grow in a way that feels right for them, and even to run without them. Some of our clients are able to work just two to three days a week and still help a lot of people because we change the way they reach people.

Another mistake many practitioners make when trying to grow their practice is focusing on how to make the phone ring. But there are actually several steps in the process that must happen before the phone will ring. Our Consistent Patients Formula for Introverts walks them through each of the steps in the right sequential order so that they have growth. We've seen clients grow even doubling or tripling in a short time frame. It's so rewarding.

## My Gift for You

It can feel challenging as an introvert, growing a business in this extroverted world. I wrote a book for holistic practitioners called The Introvert's Advantage: A Simple Blueprint System to Fill a Practice with Less Marketing.

It teaches some common misconceptions about what defines an introvert and an extrovert. It gives top marketing strategies for introverts, so you don't always have to force yourself to be "out there." Finally, it offers very practical tips that you can use right away to bring more patients into your practice, such as how to develop relationships with medical doctors so they refer their patients to you.

Grab your gift from Chen Yen at:
www.SuperwomanBook.com/gifts

## My Advice for You in Your Journey

Never give up on your dream or your passion. Even if it feels challenging. Even if I you don't know how it will work. Even if you go through ups and downs. Those ups and downs are actually a way for you to expand and grow.

The more you're able to express yourself fully, live your purpose, and be fulfilled, the more peace and joy you will have. So follow your heart, whatever that looks like for you. Be in a place of trusting, receiving, and noticing yourself. What are you saying yes to? Are you saying yes to trust? Are you saying yes to faith? Or are you saying yes to fear? Just follow your heart.

The more you're able to
express yourself fully,
live your purpose, and be
fulfilled, the more peace
and joy you will have.

~ Chen Yen

# I SNUCK INTO THE RADIO STATION
## I am on purpose and living my life fully.

*Raven Glover*

## My Superwoman Breakthrough

I'm so excited to share exactly how I went from being very overwhelmed, frustrated, disappointed, with a lot of highs and lows to really discovering my passion, my purpose and the reason for me being here and doing what I do.

In 2006 my dream found me at the IC unit of the hospital while I was waiting for my mother to get well. That's when I heard the voice inside me guide me and say, "It's time for you to step up, show up and grow up. It's time to look towards the future instead of just living day to day. It's time to look at what you see, and how you can serve because your mother's going to need you in a big way."

You can't help her at $10 an hour working twenty hours a week. It's time for you to do something that's going to help you, help your mom and help others along the way.

I got frustrated because I had no idea what I was going to do. I heard this message loud and clear, but I wasn't sure what I was going to do.

I always had the talent of selling and at that time I was fifty-five years old and they were letting people my age go for younger people, so I had to pick up a phone and call businesses in the phone book and offer my services.

Then, I happened to be on a conference call at the hospital with Alex Mandosian, my mentor, and he said the quickest way to become an expert is to interview experts. In that moment, it spoke to me.

As a kid at thirteen years old, I remember that I used to sneak into the local radio station. That dream was always buried inside in of me, I just didn't know how to do it.

And he said, you could go out and interview people. You don't have to be an expert, you can interview experts, you can be the Oprah in your niche. And I loved Oprah and I loved talking. I had a gift of gab and I said I could do this.

I began the journey. I got very frustrated along the way because my mother was in and out of surgery. We didn't know if she was going to make it. My sister and I were fighting because my sister kept saying, why are you so passionate about doing this? We don't even know if mom's going to make it. What are you talking about a radio show? I pushed past that pain to get to my power.

Long story short, the way I had to do that was go back to basics, so to speak. I took a piece of paper and I drew a line down the middle. One side was what I needed to do and then on the other side I wrote where to begin.

Then, I just did a brain dump. I didn't think about it. I got out of my head and got into my heart. That's what I now tell my clients to do too because our head gets us stuck.

Before I knew it, I had drafted out every step, and written down my show. I knew it was going to be for baby boomer women, just like me, who wanted more out of life and were determined to get it. That's how I moved forward past my overwhelm, frustration and self-doubt was by getting into action. I got out my head and into my heart and discovered what my purpose was. It worked for me and it works for many of my clients today.

## My Tools & Rituals to Stay in the Flow

I have a mantra I think about often of "Don't wait to be great, do it now". I realized by watching my mom in the Intensive Care Unit at that time, she was over seventy years old and she walked in there looking like Lena Horne, a beautiful woman, always dressed, just took good care of herself and just like that—it was taken away.

She ended up being in a wheelchair. You could see her bones and her independence was taken away. She couldn't even go to the restroom on her own and had to use a catheter, but she still fought. I remember my mom taking a stick around the house, and she tied things on it and she would reach to get things and still be very independent.

She still dressed up every day. I remember we used to tease her about putting a glitter on her wheelchair. She was still going to be fashionable and look as best she could, no matter the situation she was in. What I learned from her was, your circumstances do not define who you are and what you do to live your life.

I learned to focus and make my intention each and every day—to get more life out of living and more living out a life. That means get rid of the complaining, and deal with the pain or anything that you're dealing with. My pastor used to say the good book says, "Though I walk through the valley…", not sit, pull up a chair and drink a beer.

Those are some of the things I do to keep me going. I'm from the old school, maybe you can tell. I'm a survivor every day getting the most out of it and I keep going forward. I really don't mind failing forward. Do I get frustrated? Yes.

Sometimes I have my good cry, scream and yell. In fact, I have the ugly cry, but then afterwards you have to be able to get back up.

You have to move forward. It's okay. It's not the end of life. That's what I hold on to, the fact that I get to wake up every day. I'm still here. I can still pursue my dreams and sadly many cannot, because there are many out there whose dreams were cut short. Many dreams were never even born because they lost their life, so how dare I stay in the pain of whatever I'm dealing with now, I have to push past it and move forward because I'm still here.

Zig Ziglar says, if you help enough people get what they want, you'll get what you want. I remember that and get past my pain and focus on how I can serve others. I focus on showing them how to use the power of their voice and their heartfelt message and sprinkle it with some amazing kick ass interviews.

## My Purpose Is

I support women by showing them how they can be free to be them. Be free to take your heartfelt message and don't worry about what others are going to say. Just get it out to the world because someone is looking for you to be the leader and they can't find you because they don't know where you are.

I help you find your voice and sometimes it's not even finding your voice, but it's in having someone to say, yes, you need to be heard.

Your message needs to be heard. I help people identify what their message is and how they want to present it. Some people don't want to do video, and some people don't want to do TV. Others feel very comfortable about being behind the mic on audio. Some feel very comfortable about live streaming. We find out what platform is good for you and then I help you to become an Oprah or the Larry King in your niche.

I love helping people to interview because anyone can start there. You don't have to worry about if you're an expert or know enough, or if you have enough content. You can simply go out there and interview the great people out there, the ones who are your heroes, who are your Sheroes to get started. We make a list of their heroes and Sheroes and then we show them how to pursue them the right way and get those interviews. I teach them how to ask for and conduct the interview.

I teach them how to ask for the money, honey, because once you interview, you want to turn that interview into a cash machine. Then I teach them how to market their interview and how to slice that interview, just like my mom used to do with that good old sweet potato pies and how sweet it is, and then we show them how to package it.

I show them how to build a business around being a talk show host and interviewing other people as an extension of their business and it becomes a marketing tool.

## My Gift for You

My gift is the Interview Profit Secrets Masterclass training with a group of amazing women featured. You will see how we showed them to how easy it is to start their interviews, because that's where most people get stuck.

I teach my audience, and you'll hear this in the course, that even though it's a kitchen table or you're doing the show or the interview from your bedroom or wherever you're doing it, you want to come to the mic with the mindset of being on CNN, CBS, MSNBC. You want to stand into that power because you can reach millions of people around the world. In the training, we also cover how to get the interviews, where to find those people and how to drip on them. You don't want to make the mistake and just charge at them, we show how to follow them, and what you can do to create a win-win.

I teach how to present the opportunity of being on your show or doing the interview for you, or your summit and present it in a way that's a win, win, win—a win for you, a win for them and a win for your audience.

Then we talk about what to do with those interviews. I see so many people have interviews on their hard drive like summits, shows and podcasts and that's a lot of money sitting there you can leverage. It's a great training overall so I'm excited to offer it as a gift for you.

Grab your gift from Raven Glover at: www.SuperwomanBook.com/gifts

## My Advice for You in Your Journey

My advice is to wake up every day counting the blessings that you've been given. Focus your intention each and every moment of the day to get more life out of living and more living out a life. Just go for it. Live your life. You'll live your life free when you focus on what you're here to do. We're all here for a reason, so be purpose driven and stay in action.

Wake up every day counting the blessings that you've been given. Just go for it. Live your life.

~ Raven Glover

# TRUSTING MY OWN VOICE AGAIN

I am healing. I am connected to my truth.

*Melyssa Moniz*

## My Superwoman Breakthrough

2018 was a massive year of problems and challenges, one after another. I hadn't seen life so packed with challenges like that for quite some time.

As a serial entrepreneur, I create several different content packages. I do a lot of different work for other entrepreneurs to help them build their brands and build themselves. But in 2018, I found myself behind the scenes, crumbling in the background and wondering what the heck was going on.

I felt like a fraud, and that little "fraud voice" in the back of my head started to eat away at me. It felt like an internal dying, like the last remnants of this old self who thought, "I have to be perfect. I have to be this, I have to be that." The "I have to" voice got really strong and loud. I couldn't hear my usual authentic, inspired voice, anymore.

I rejected and negated a lot of my usual principles. So, internally, I started to decompose. I felt like I was dying on the inside.

At one point, I got really sick; bedridden. My energy levels were extremely depleted, and I had no appetite; I kept vomiting and I couldn't get out of bed.

That lasted for almost twelve weeks straight. I couldn't work, so I didn't have the usual cash flow or cash injections coming in. Money seemed like the be all, and end all… and I was hitting an ultimate low in my bank account.

I felt this loud panicking. Then I started to realize, "I need to get the heck out of this."

I ignored all the sick feelings. I didn't "feel" one hundred percent, but I said, "I have to be better." I started to crawl out of bed.

Soon, I got a car. I hadn't had a car for a little while. I'd been relying on Uber, planes, trains, taxi cabs—living the jet-set life and not driving my own vehicle. However, I had this inner craving, like an old part of me was saying, "No, I want to get back to driving. I want to be the driver of my own life again." My inner self was urging me to just get it done and take the action that I was urging myself to do.

I started to drive a little bit recklessly though. I'm normally a very responsible person, but suddenly I started being very irresponsible—speeding and texting while driving. I started to put myself at risk because of an internal, fearful voice that said, "You have to hurry up because you're supposed to be further ahead. Hurry up! Hurry up!"

I started to do contract work again—work that was outside of my genius zone, below my pay grade level, and beneath my entrepreneurial spirit. I knew that, but I did it anyway because I was chasing money. It hurt my ego, but my soul reminded me that I was going to be ok. I listened to the voice that said, "I have to hurry up and get more money coming in."

So much pressure... The pressure that I was so used to in an old version of myself... But the work wasn't fulfilling. The companies I contracted with didn't want to hear anything that I had to say from an innovative standpoint. They didn't want to hear my opinion or learn from my experience. I was struggling. There was quite a bit of resistance in terms of communication.

People in the rat-race world are silenced, in many ways, and that had always turned me off. I mean no disrespect to anyone who chooses that pathway, however for me, I did not realize that the ability to make quick and nourishing decisions was such a privilege within entrepreneurship. I was starting to realize what I was taking for granted, and where I was ungrateful in my life.

In one corporation I contracted with during this time, the executive board and some of my colleagues even verbally abused me. They created a lot of toxicity in the background and from the executive chain of communication. They said and did things on purpose just to try to trip me up. I'm a tough-skinned person, but their behavior was fundamentally wrong. I had forgotten bullying still exists.

I had to learn how to start speaking eloquently, out of love. I came to a place of, "Here I am, and if you're not okay with that, I'm not going to reflect the same negative energy. This will not be war. I choose better for myself."

I just couldn't do it anymore. I had every right to take legal action, but I decided not to continue the negative vibe.

Thankfully, the contract was terminated cleanly and quickly. I took that as a sign from the universe listening to my loud, persistent requests for transformation.

But then I faced another hardship.

I live in Ontario, Canada, and we had some crazy weather at that time. One day it snowed; the next day it was sunny. As I drove to the store location where I'd be working one day, a mixture of ice and rain began to fall. Within twenty minutes, the road was covered in black ice; it was slippery and dangerous.

All of a sudden, I saw a car stopped in the middle of the highway a few hundred meters in front of me. I pumped my brakes, but I crashed into him. I felt furious when I got out of the car. I was on the brink of screaming at the top of my lungs until I saw that the other driver was an elderly man.

He looked clearly confused, and also scared. I had a weird moment of compassion mixed with happiness that I was alive, and anger that nothing was wrong with him. I wondered, "Why is it my car that's all banged up now and not his? How is this possible?"

I'd just been bedridden for twelve weeks. I had all these contracts lined up because I finally owned a car to drive to them. But then I totaled my car. I knew in that moment, "That stuff's not panning out."

At the sound of my car crashing in front of another car, on a dangerous, life-threatening moment, all these thoughts and feelings happened in one moment.

It woke me up.

I had this massive amount of turmoil in my life: life aches, money aches, and now body aches from the accident. Everything ached!

The internal judgments started coming. I journaled them all out, writing down the voices that told me, "You're a failure. You lost your car; you lost this; you lost that. You're never going to have more money coming in. You're worthless"

I realized that none of that was true; it was all B.S., and I had to get the garbage out.

I realized that I did, in fact, know better. I did hear my authentic voice, though I'd ignored it far too long.

I said, "I'm done with this."

I could feel all these different things inside of me telling me, "Come on already. You know the truth, so live the truth." I felt like a snake shedding its skin.

Days and days of healing began to unfold.

I started tapping back into the rituals that I know from the Law of Attraction, from my spirituality, from my core being.

The insurance company gave me a fair lump sum of cash, which was a godsend.

I had another little bout of bedridden sickness again. I went to the doctor and found out that my adrenal glands were shot and that my vitamin levels were quite off. My body had been going through a lot of changes and I had ignored the signs. I decided to not ignore them anymore. So I got back in tune with my rituals and began the healing journey of my mind, body and soul yet again. I started paying attention again. I went out dancing and I enrolled in thirty days of yoga in order to get back in touch with my body, which I had been ignoring for so long.

When my focus shifted, and I began to see clearly, feel clearly and feel better, I also realized that I did have many things working in my life, like my e-book which was about to be published.

I started to pay attention to the things that actually made my heart sing. I feel like mountains have moved underneath me, through me, over me, and around me.

As of today, I feel like I have a clear slate. I know very well by now that my life will continue to show my challenges on the way to my life's most meaningful experiences. And I feel more equipped than ever to take on every challenge that comes my way.

## My Tools & Rituals to Stay in the Flow

Rituals are very important because the same brain that came up with one problem is still the same brain that will come up with a solution. Creativity is a powerful way to access divine inspiration. Rituals leverage our naturally-occurring rhythms and encourage us to focus deeply on the elements of our being that cause harmony, health and happiness. I have been practicing since a very young age and continue to teach and mentor others who desire to be in their authentic flow as well.

However, I have to be careful about the input I receive, because my output is directly impacted by the input. That's not just for me; that's for everybody. If we pay attention to too much input that isn't ours by intention—i.e. noise from people's judgments, from society, from mass marketing, social media, etc.—it's hard to hear your own whispers.

Inspiration often comes in a whisper. It's not a loud blaring. I had to learn how to dissolve the noise. The brain is so sophisticated. You can actually pick and choose your neural pathways. Take a moment to imagine the internet. Consider, the internet was created as a mirror image of how our brain actually works. Fascinating.

Even though I am aware I am still evolving, and still on the journey, I decided my role as a service-based, creative entrepreneur was to utilize my life as a platform to experiment with human potential. I always start with myself as the guinea pig.

So, several years ago, I became a registered hypnotherapist. I learned how to hypnotize myself to transcend into a frequency and a vibration of how I was when I was first born. This is actually the frequency of the planet.

When we come to harmonize and connect to that frequency, suddenly we're on a new vibration and we can access other information, other parts of our brain, and other parts of our bodies. We can effectively tap into, and live, our potential.

We can start to create what's called Coherence. That's when the hearts' intention and your brain's intention actually correlate and bring everything together. That's when we step into a totally different way of being. We start hearing feedback like people saying, "There's just this aura about you." This is when the majority of your life feels authentic to you and flows towards the desires you authentically wish to experience in your lifetime.

## How I Help You

I help people step into their self-expression, authentically and powerfully. I resonate most with other creators, so I help

The Superwoman Entrepreneur

them create a brand that is an extension of them. Brand elements such as the signature experience, key colours and the visual essence of what they want to represent in the world. I utilize my mastery in both verbal and non-verbal communication to tap into my client's truth and help them create an actionable plan they are self-motivated to execute and live into. These are intentional practices.

After seventeen years of both offline and online business, I've mastered the ability to translate these elements quickly into a brand that has you living into that brand experience more often than not.

An elevated level of service that I bring to my clients now is the self-care that is necessary for high impact, performance-oriented, experience-oriented individuals—which tends to be a lot of female entrepreneurs as of today. It's all about the lifestyle. Lastly, coordinating dream teams for my clients to help them delegate and grow their capacity to serve without becoming a workaholic. This is perhaps the most satisfying part of the whole process!

It's also all about having true impact—the way I see it, we only have ONE life that we know of in this precious moment of now, and I love the impact building brands and businesswomen has in our lifetime.

## My Gift for You

The gift is called Six Steps to Master Your Personal Brand. It is a simple set of questions that when you engage with, it reveals your foundation for a brand that you will love to share with your ideal clients. Here's to getting you started on a beautiful (and challenging) process meant to bring you prosperity—the way you imagined.

Grab your gift from Melyssa Moniz at: www.SuperwomanBook.com/gifts

## My Advice for You in Your Journey

Trust yourself. Trust that the universe truly wants to give you anything and everything you request. Trust that you are in the right spot at the right time. Trust that even when it's ugly, it's beautiful

Trust that the universe truly wants to give you anything and everything you request.

~ Melyssa Moniz

# EMOTIONAL LEADERSHIP
I am a leader who is in touch with my emotions.

*Andrea J. Lee*

## My Superwoman Breakthrough

When I was eighteen, I had a really pivotal experience which played a big part in the kind of leader I am today. It was a very unpleasant experience, but it turned out to be a deep leadership lesson.

I was on vacation with my family. Legally blind, my brother Eddie, was sitting on his bed, wearing his thick black glasses with fingerprints all over the lenses.

My dad, a high-achieving, overburdened immigrant carrying the weight of the world on his shoulders, suddenly become very angry with Eddie. Things happened very quickly. In his anger, my dad raised his hand to hit my brother. That moment seemed to freeze, and the voice inside my head said,

"Dad, you're not going to hit Eddie are you? No, you can't hit Eddie! Dad, you can't hit Eddie!"

And I hit my dad instead. Well, I shoved him. Hard. Right in the chest.

After I started breathing again, I realized my Dad had left the room. Eddie was back to whatever he was doing. Things had—at least on the surface—returned back to normal, whatever normal was.

But in that moment, something had changed. It wasn't at the level of consciousness yet, but since that day I've done a lot of thinking and this is what I want to share with you. That moment was important because it was the moment I stopped being a victim, and instead, I went all the way to the other end of the spectrum and became an aggressor. I got a taste of power, and I liked it.

In later years, I embraced that feeling of aggression, and it took me a long time to recover from this inappropriate anger, and the emotional violence I was creating in my closest relationship. So even though it was out of protection of my brother, and even though it would be easy to think I had triumphed in that moment of hitting my Dad, it was actually a crossroads that led to some of the darkest moments in my life. I had to wrestle with my inner anger and abuse of anger.

Why do I share this story with you? I believe that as women, we have a lot of unearthed power inside of us. We spend a lot of our lives being victims, especially in our emotional lives. We're either too nice, or we're bitches. Too complaint, or too much 'like a man'. When we finally express our feelings, they come out in extremes. It's partially because they've been pent up and stored for too long. It's partially because we don't know how to use our anger in constructive ways. All of this leads to a blunting of our power and a dulling of our joy.

Our good power—our right power—lives between victimhood and aggression. Learning to wield our right power, and express it in our work, in our relationships, and with our family—this is an amazing goal I wish more women would embrace! When we know how to live well with all of our emotions, we become fluent in emotional leadership.

As an entrepreneur, my best days—the best launches, the best partnerships, the projects that succeed and earn the most money—are all sourced from that middle powerful place between being a victim and being an aggressor.

Use team building as an example. Anybody who is building a bigger business will need to reflect on the kind of leader they are for the team that they're building. I often say that a business only grows to the size of the owner's leadership. What that means is, if your emotional leadership is lacking, you will have difficulty attracting, and keeping a team. When this is true, your team will keep breaking apart around you until you sort out how to break the cycle of emotional upheaval.

Would an example help here, perhaps? Well, in one of my previous businesses, there was a person on my sales team who would not provide the reports that I expected, even though I clearly communicated her responsibility to do so. On the victim side of the emotional spectrum, I could have put up with this because she did most of her job right and handled my need for reports some other way. On the aggressor side of the emotional spectrum, I could have become furious—perhaps verbally abusive—and fired her on the spot without hearing her side.

In this case, however, I was able to choose the middle ground. I consulted with my advisors and coaches, and then took the time to tell her very clearly, "I need these reports. If you cannot do these reports, then this isn't the right fit. This is not the right job for you and you're not right for this company."

## My Tools & Rituals to Stay in the Flow

Understand that your emotions are part of your toolbox. Emotional leadership is just like any other kind of mastery. Be conscious of your tools, practice with them, invest in keeping them sharp, and most of all use them! Denying that you have emotions is not going to make them go away.

We may think of ourselves as super women and entrepreneurs. We're leaders for sure. But very rarely do we talk about our emotions, even though they're with us just like our skin.

Remember that this starts with feeling your feelings fully. If you're repressing your feelings, it will be impossible for you to lead from the heart.

## My Purpose Is

I consider myself to be a leadership coach for anyone who's trying to change or shift the culture.

Maribel is creating a change to ensure that entrepreneurs have peace, play, and prosperity—not just one of them, but all three. Other entrepreneurs have a social activist bent in their business. Those are examples of making a shift in culture.

I work a lot with emotional abuse cycles. I have some groups and, of course, my books. But most of my work is done privately, and in intimate groups, where leaders can tell their secrets about the emotions they've been feeling—and usually repressing—for a long time.

They haven't had a safe place to speak about their emotions before—to honor them as part of the toolbox. And because of that, these leaders are less powerful than they can be. They're working with half a deck of cards. They're trying to use their brains and their minds to drive their businesses. But when the heart comes on board and partners with the mind, that's very powerful. I help them free the heart so it can partner with the mind and drive the success of their business or project.

## My Gift for You

My gift is an almost-monthly community coaching call that's complimentary.

We gather on an online tool called Zoom. Because I like to walk my talk, each call I teach something that is very much on my heart and my mind. It's always something current and immediately useful. Then we have a Q&A with coaching spotlights so you can receive support for something you're contending with, whatever it is at that moment.

Grab your gift from Andrea J. Lee at: www.SuperwomanBook.com/gifts

## My Advice for You in Your Journey

Create a practice where you develop a relationship with your emotions. You can start right now if you like. Just close your eyes for a moment and think about your emotions. Welcome them into the circle with you as friends, allies, and partners—champions of your life and your work.

Sometimes you might notice anger front and center. You could try saying, "Hey Anger, how's it going? Oh, I see you're really upset today."

For sadness or grief, you could say, "Hey, I get that things are down today. Come on in, have a comfy seat, tell me what's up."

Of course, there are many other ways to become fluent with your emotions, and to infuse your leadership with a greater resilience and power. But especially if you've been dealing with inappropriate anger or other emotions for a long time, you need baby steps at first. Over time, you can begin to create a team between you and your emotions.

From this, all kinds of results will show up. And the best thing is that you're doing and your being will be aligned. There is no greater joy than playing full out in your aligned power.

This is my wish for you.

There is no greater joy
than playing full out in
your aligned power.

~Andrea J. Lee

# FROM TEEN MOM TO BUSINESS OWNER
## I am strong.

*Florine Hall*

## My Superwoman Breakthrough

I was sixteen years old when I had my son. I got very sick and spent the last week of my pregnancy in the hospital. The doctors had actually prepared my family for the worst. I imagined my mom, watching her daughter go through such a terrible situation at sixteen years old, and having to decide if something happened, whether to save her daughter's life or her grandchild's life.

I don't really remember much about that time in the hospital. I do remember seeing people I hadn't seen for a very long time. I knew something was wrong. I just didn't know what.

At one point, the voices got very faint. I remember hearing buzzers/loud machines, and then the next thing I remember is seeing nurses next to me. My vision was pretty blurry, but I can slightly hear someone say, "Enise, can you hear me? We have your son here. He has been placed in an incubator for transport to the children's hospital. You can open the side and touch him if you like as we really need to move him quickly." I remember someone leaving to get my mom, and then the whole team surround me, checking me out.

All was a blur at this point by I do remember my mom telling me that I'd been out of it for a few days. My son had been born via an emergency C-section at thirty-two weeks. I found out that my liver almost burst, and my kidneys were shutting down and failing very quickly. I remember my first night at the hospital, before things became such a blur, staff putting eleven IV bags in my system in one night.

I lost so much weight during my pregnancy. I weighed ninety-six pounds by the time I was hospitalized. I couldn't hold down any food. The only thing my son had to get nutrients from was my blood, which wasn't very good due to the anemia. He weighed three pounds and three and a half ounces when he was born.

He was in the children's hospital for six weeks. When he weighed four and a half pounds, the doctors released him to come home. Over the next few months, I noticed that he wasn't crawling like he should have been. After tons of testing, he was diagnosed with cerebral palsy at eight months of age. I didn't know what that was, so I had to learn. He had tons of therapy appointments, as well as multiple neurology appointments and surgeries along the way.

Eventually, I found the United Cerebral Palsy Foundation, which became one of my support systems. They taught me about cerebral palsy and all the things that could come with it.

My mom was my rock through everything. I came from a single-family home, and there I was, a single mom myself.

Then, my son started having seizures. They were very silent. I had to physically look at him to know that he was seizing. As time passed, I learned that he couldn't get too hot, or too cold, or he would seize. Every little noise that he made, or sound throughout the house, I was up, making sure he was okay. Lots of sleepless nights and long days. This was a lot for me at that time so work, college, I had to stop everything to care for my son.

After taking off two years to try and understand the lifestyle we had, trying to get the seizures under control, and I finally was able to go back to work.

I began working retail, about thirty hours a week, in this timeframe, I was able to meet a nice guy who had a daughter of his own. We became a family, and that relationship lasted about sixteen years.

After my husband and I parted ways, my son's seizures got worse. He started having grand mal seizures, which were very severe. Once, he regurgitated while he was seizing and the food reversed, filling up one of his lungs. He wasn't getting oxygen. His skin tone was changing colors. My friend, Cynthia, had to take me away so the paramedics could take care of him.

I found myself in a paralyzed mindset, like I was paralyzed along with my son. The doctors had told me when I was younger that, based on his health, he probably would only live to the age of ten years old. Being in my own space wasn't really my priority. I was just trying to survive, and to spend as much time with him as I possibly could.

But I took strength from my family and my faith. I always knew that I wanted to become a business owner of some sort. And when I was thirty-five, I took my life back. I realized, "I know who God created. I am a firecracker. Knowing who I am, he would have not given me this little boy just to take him away from me. He's going to outlive me."

That realization pushed me to pursue my education again. I enrolled back in school, and now this is where my fifty hours weeks began. I graduated in four years with my bachelor's degree, all while handling my son's full schedule of medical appointments.

Slowly, my son's seizures stopped. He's now an adult. He's wheelchair bound and wears diapers. We have to feed him and care for him—the whole bit. But when people take the time to know him, they fall in love with him. He has such a fun personality, loves music and likes when people talk to him. When he gets his haircut, he has his demeanor like, "Okay mom, I'll cool right now. I'm cute. You can't talk to me right now." He is something else.

I am remarried and my husband now, who was my friend for about ten years, was the missing piece I needed. I had no clue that I would marry him. But when my son met him, they had an instant connection. My son doesn't do that to anyone. I knew that something was different. I found out later that he was once the house manager of a disabled group home. I think my son probably felt that warmth from him.

When the two of them are in a room together, I don't even exist. My son acts like, "Yeah, I know he's your husband, Mom, but he's now my bonus dad." You could not tell my son that that man isn't his father.

Even though life has been a whirlwind, I would do it all again. I believe that I ended up where I am today because I never lost my true focus. I never lost my faith in God. I had the help of my family and my friends. And I always tried to stay positive through everything that happened.

Of course, I had days when I felt sorry for myself, and I asked tons of questions. I didn't want to question God, but we're only human when we have those questions. I shed a lot of tears and said a lot of prayers. Ultimately, my faith got me through it.

## My Tools & Rituals to Stay in the Flow

I stay peaceful by never underestimating what God has planned for me.

You could have all the plans in the world for yourself, but he will remind you who's really in charge. When you realize the strength that God has given you, he will put you out there. You will either sink or swim.

Knowing where my strength comes from, and staying humble about that, keeps me in the flow.

I also have peace knowing that I have a husband who loves me unconditionally. Together, we run a Jamaican food business that keeps me sane, believe it or not. It's a lot of hard work, but I feel such peace when we're running our food business and I'm talking to families and helping them find some peace of their own.

## My Purpose Is

I love mentoring individuals. So often, people just want someone to listen to them—not so much to give them advice, but just to listen to them. They may have their friends and family, but sometimes it's more helpful when they have a complete stranger who will let them do all the talking. I like to do that.

I love supporting women, especially. We all have our roles in our relationships with our spouses. They always say, "Behind every great man is a strong woman." I think they need to be next to each other because we all play a role. There is no 50/50. There's 100/100 across the board.

## My Gift for You

My gift is "Tips on Busting Through the Unknown: From Teen Mom to Business Owner". We all have our own journey and you have no idea where life will take you. But when you keep a level head and you know where you want to go, you will get there. You may go through different obstacles. You may go backwards a few times. But you will definitely get there. You'd have to stay focused because you cannot lose your train of thought.

Grab your gift from Florine Hall at: www.SuperwomanBook.com/gifts

## My Advice for You in Your Journey

Never give up. You never want to look back in life and say, "I wish I would have." The entire process of getting my degree took seventeen years. That's a very long time to not lose hope. But you must have faith, remain humble. I remember hearing a pastor on the radio say Life is a battlefield. God will put you in that battlefield and it is up to you to come out on the other side. I feel like once I realized the strength I was given, I needed to go in that battlefield and use all of my tools and resources to bring me out. I do this daily, doesn't matter how much things can appear to be great, you still will have a battle you will need to fight to own it and rejoice in this ride.

Also, you're always going to have bills and other things come up in your life. Unfortunate circumstances happen. But you won't always be there to see your family grow. So every chance you possibly can, grab ahold of your family. They are sacred valuables that you don't want to take advantage of. Live that part as often as you can.

Every chance you possibly
can, grab ahold of your
family. They are sacred
valuables that you don't
want to take advantage
of.

~ Florine Hall

# EMBRACING WHO I AM
## I am in the flow.

*Kaayla Vedder*

## My Superwoman Breakthrough

I've learned that, when you're in flow, life is easy. It's simple. But when you don't recognize your guidance and you allow yourself to be in the ego instead of the flow, you put on the brakes. You say things like, "I'm not enough. I could never do that anyway." All these limiting beliefs come up. When you try to muscle your way through stuff, it's exhausting.

There have been numerous times in my life where I've been forced to stop, like a cosmic two-by-four smacked me down so that I have to actually stop and listen for that guidance.

Before I had children, I worked with street-entrenched youth. I felt exhausted, confused, overwhelmed. I knew that it was time for me to move on and do something different. I could feel the universe guiding me, but I didn't listen. I lived in fear. First of all, I worried about what they would do without me. It was totally my ego. Then, I worried about what I would do next. So I hesitated. I stayed. Then I got taken out. I became very ill and had to do some serious self-care and some deep-diving into myself in order to listen to that guidance.

I got an amazing job in the corporate world doing sales. One night, I was working very late. My boss reached out to me and asked, "What are you doing?" I told him I was doing my reports. He said, "Yeah, I see that. I just got one of them. Why are you doing it now? It's ten o'clock at night."

I said, "I need to clear my plate because I've got more sales coming." I felt the need to go, go, go.

My boss said, "You need to just stop for a minute. Take a whole day off. Take your kids somewhere for a nice meal and write it off and send me the receipts."

It was such a beautiful gift.

Right away, my ego responded, "My kids are little; we don't do nice dinners."

He said, "I don't care if you take them to Chuck E Cheese. Just go."

I had a hard time receiving the gifts that presented themselves to me. I was in so much fear of putting bread on the table, making sure there was a roof over our heads, and making sure that I had more than enough to not just survive but thrive.

I started to do some work with myself to get more comfortable in my own skin. As I started listening to the guidance, many more things opened up to me.

I remember sitting down in the middle of my living room of my rented house one day. It wasn't a very nice house, to be honest, but I'd put out to the universe that I wanted a place which I could easily afford. I felt so overwhelmed with the responsibility of changing the space into something beautiful, embracing what I had, and moving forward with this job.

I just cried and cried and cried. I felt such a release. And when I did that, I called in to the universe and asked for assistance. I said, "Just show me." And things started to change. I had to be willing to release a lot of stuff—a lot of shame, a lot of "not enough," a lot of "you can't do this."

When my kids were younger, my mom had an amazing practice of healing work. She was a trailblazer. Unfortunately, she got injured, and I had to call some of her clients to cancel their appointments.

One of her clients asked me, "So what do you do?"

I said, "What makes you think I do anything?"

He said, "I can feel it."

I said, "I don't do anything like what she does. I don't actually need you in my presence. It's very different."

He said, "I'd like to book a session with you. Do you have any time available on Saturday?"

I don't even know where the words came from, but I said, "I'll have to check my schedule and get back to you." I shared this conversation with my family. I told them, "This isn't for me." I came up with all the excuses.

My husband said, "Do you remember when you mentioned a month ago that you wanted a massage table and you didn't know why? It arrived today. I set it up downstairs."

Talk about being divinely guided and nudged in a big way!

So I called the client. I was so nervous. He didn't answer and I felt relieved that I didn't have to talk to him. I thought, "Well, he's not getting an appointment. This is perfect."

My youngest daughter looked at me and said, "Mom, I don't know what you're getting all worked up about. Just be you, and do what you do."

So I called again and booked his appointment. That was the beginning of me stepping more into who I am and why I'm here. I never advertised, I built my practice on word of mouth as I became more open to working on people other than my close friends and family.

Then I kept following my guidance. One client suggested that I do meditation, and offered to host it at her house. And meditation nights were born. I kept following those nudges, that guidance, letting myself be me and allowing the chips to fall where they may.

Along the way, I learned that, when you start to embrace your gifts, you get really excited. The fear starts to go away. You realize that you can help people, and you start talking about it. You learn as you go. You must be willing to step into the unknown. Learn how to listen to your guidance. It's always there.

## My Tools & Rituals to Stay in the Flow

When I decided to embrace who I am, I took advantage of any and every free thing available. I tuned in to see if it felt like a fit. If it didn't fit, that was okay. I took what felt right and left the rest behind.

We can learn tools and glean wisdom from other people's experiences. But we're each on our own individual journey. We each have our own unique gifts, our own purpose, and our own contribution to humanity.

When I completely surrender to divine source, and get out of my own way and say, "Just show me," the most beautiful things happen.

We all see, feel, and experience things in different ways. No matter what it is, you can't get it wrong. When your mind is chit-chatting, it's a sign that you are trying to guide the boat versus going along with the flow of the water.

If it is in the highest, as soon as you move energy on it, it's going to grow legs and take off. But if you try to muscle your way into something, it's going to be hard. It's going to be a struggle. You will feel resistance. You will know.

You're always being guided to what's in the highest for you. Recognize that, ask, and be willing to receive—without wanting an instantaneous result. You can place your order with the universe, but it might take a little while to cook and prepare everything in perfect synchronicity. There are a lot of moving parts to coordinate. If things don't come together in your timing, it will come together in divine timing. It may not be in the highest right at this moment.

Remember that if it feels difficult, like you're pushing through things, you're in your ego. When you're in flow, opportunities will present themselves.

One of the tools I picked up is to ask, "How can it get any better than this? What else is possible?" When you play with those questions, you will not believe the things that show up for you. It just keeps growing into more and more juicy deliciousness when you open yourself up for something new and different to arrive.

And what if things are absolutely amazing? Ask the same question. Open up to even more.

Learn to let go of an instantaneous response and trust in the flow and the guidance that is already there for you. Release some of those limiting beliefs and entanglements that you may not even know are running in the background, keeping you stuck. They affect you physically, mentally, emotionally, spiritually.

Setting intentions is another important tool for me. Every morning before I arise, I tune into the feeling that something amazing will happen that day. Like a kid right before Christmas, I have this goofy anticipation of wondering what form it will take. I set that intention and then go on about my day.

Recently, I set the intention of joy, fun, and playfulness on a hike I took with a friend. We hiked to an outlook at the end of the trail. Everything was lovely. As we headed back, and I looked off the path and saw a swing in the middle of the bushes.

Now, I didn't see this swing on our way in. I walked this trail many times and I had never seen a swing before. So the next thing you know, we were swinging like a couple of kids, in the middle of a forest. We had so much fun.

That is the power of intention. I don't know who put that swing up. I don't know how long it was there. Maybe it manifested just for us. I have no idea, and I don't care. I'm just grateful.

When you set an intention first thing in the morning, you never know what will happen.

This concept works even when things aren't going well. Let yourself feel whatever it is. If you're going to have a crappy day, make it the best crappiest day ever. Dive deep, roll around in it, feel sorry for yourself, do the whole pity party. Invite some friends if you want to. Let yourself have it.

I guarantee that the decision to let yourself have the crappiest day ever will shift the energy. Suddenly, it becomes funny, even ridiculous. Before you know it, you'll be laughing. You'll realize that it was just your ego trying to keep you safe.

We can get really serious with our ego. So let it have its little hissy fit. When you're really honest with yourself, you'll find it laughable. You'll see how much you're digging in your heels when the universe is guiding you to let go of something old that's running in the background.

## My Purpose Is

Diamond Consciousness is the new energy that's coming in. I've learned a lot of different modalities on my journey. But when this new energy came in, I was guided to let go of a lot of the old ways that came from a place of fear and safety. So I assist people to step into this new energy by releasing the cell memory from lifetimes and the entanglements of their energies.

Imagine that you take your computer into the shop and you say, "I don't know why, but I can't seem to run this new program."

The tech looks at it and says, "Oh my gosh. It's because you have 500 bazillion things running in the background that you can't even see."

You ask, "So, do I need those?"

The tech says, "No. They don't even match up with what's happening in the world today." So he deletes all the old programs.

That's what I do. I delete all the old entanglements and limiting beliefs that run in the background. Then the Diamond Encodements bring in new activations and new energy, so that now you can hook up to all the new programs that are available to you.

I see all these limitations. I see all these entanglements. I've always been aware that I see and feel things in ways that others don't, like I had a muscle flexed and ready to go when I came into this physical body that I learned to use very quickly.

On occasion, I will speak to somebody who has transitioned—if it's in the highest for whomever I'm working with, or if they need that validation in order to move beyond a feeling or an emotion that's keeping them stuck.

You have all these expectations on you before you're even born. Maybe your parents were excited for your entrance into this world. They created all these beautiful expectations and wants and desires for you. When you were born, you had all those things connected to you.

If you think about it, your parents had expectations placed on them, as did your grandparents and great-grandparents. Those connections go back generations. They don't fit the energy of what is showing up right now, but they're still connected to you.

I assist you in releasing those connections and bringing in higher levels of your consciousness.

## My Gift for You

My gift is a free masterclass called 5 Keys to Living in Your Flow and Connecting with Your Own Divine Guidance.

In this masterclass, I give you five easy steps to recognize the signs and symbols that are available to assist you. It helps you live your life feeling fully supported and guided, knowing that you're heading in the right direction and that you're amazing. It's juicy.

Grab your gift from Kaala Vedder at: www.SuperwomanBook.com/gifts

## Final piece of advice

Whatever is going on in your life, it's never about the other person.

Get a piece of paper or journal. Every night before you go to bed, list five things that you're grateful for. Some days it'll simply be breathing, and that's okay.

Open yourself up to abundance. Ask yourself this question: if there was no money involved, "What would I want to do?"

Open yourself up to
abundance.

~ Kaala Vedder

# FROM CORPORATE FINANCE, TO POTTERY, TO BUSINESS PROFIT MENTOR

I am fulfilled on this adventure.

*Anne Dickinson*

## My Superwoman Breakthrough

I was in a corporate life in finance and I it wasn't fun for me.

I took what I call a left turn and I went back to school for pottery for two years and then opened a pottery studio.

The process of opening the studio and putting together the business plan and really going back to my roots of business education was so much fun for me!

The business was profitable in eighteen months and debt free in five years which is pretty unheard of for an art studio. It was just a blast doing that and I realized how much I loved it.

At the time, I was also trying to make a living with my pottery. That part was less successful and eventually five years into it, I realized I wasn't making a living with it.

There was the next breakdown—part two. I wasn't making enough from my own work to say, "Okay, I can do this for a living."

I sold my interest in the studio and then I thought what am I going to do next?

I looked back at what I had done and said to myself, wait a second—I love working with businesses. So I decided to open up what's now my business, Eye On Your Business (all puns intended). I realized my strongest skill set is in helping business owners really improve the health of their businesses and it's been so fulfilling for me.

I was seeing fellow artists not making it because they didn't understand the business stuff. The business stuff that I understand and that I love. Digging into a company and figuring out how it works is so much fun for me.

You've got people who have a passion about something, know their subject matter, and they're going to make it work no matter what. The challenge is that they don't have the business background so it becomes a real struggle over time.

I have clients who are attorneys and they're really smart people in the law but don't have the business background. It's so much fun for me to help them understand what to focus on and understand all pieces of the business.

I have the corporate finance background and the creative side that I tapped into with my pottery studio. The combination enables me to empathize with them. In my new business, I combined my artistic side, and my corporate business background with my style of being a pull no punches kind of person to get right to the heart of what will help my clients.

## My Tools & Rituals to Stay in the Flow

One of them is in-line with what I do for a living which is to keep my books in order. I make sure that I'm not in the place of, "well there's a few dollars in the bank, but I don't really understand what's going on with my business." I walk the walk.

Then from a personal standpoint, I make sure that I keep up with friends and spend time with them. I spend time outside and make sure that there are things other than business that fill my life. I like to travel, run, spend time outdoors and play with my dog.

I'm now going into another phase where I have elderly parents and that's impacting my life as well. It really is a juggling act, of helping them, keeping my business going well and keeping my own balance. I'm not perfect, but I do my best to thrive in all areas.

## My Purpose Is

I work with small business owners, to help them get more profit, and time which equates to less stress overall, and more freedom—which we all know is priceless. I do that by improving their profits, cash flow and operations. It's a process where we start by looking at their business' numbers because I know that numbers can freak people out.

I help them see where they are and then go from there with my five-step process. When you take stock of where you are and learn what your costs really are, it helps you make better business decisions. There are a lot of entrepreneurs who will just see that there's money in the bank, and therefore think they can pay their bills and that's it. There's some truth to that, but it's not an effective way to run a business.

What are fundamentally effective ways to run a business? If you are a fan of the show, The Profit with Marcus Lemonis, one of my favorites, he always talks about product, process, and people. In many respects, I do the same thing except he invests directly in the businesses. I don't have an interest in buying businesses, my mission is to help the business owner get on their own two feet

The truth is if you break down business to their most fundamental, they're the same, it's the subject matter of the company that changes. The fun part for me is figuring out the subject matter. How does a business like yours in marketing differ from that of an attorney? How can we put the pieces together in a way that is most effective for getting you further on your way? If you want a bigger company and more profit, with more cash, then understanding what you as the CEO should keep your eye on going forward is very important.

## My Gift for You

I have a great gift for business owners to get started, it's called a Business Freedom Scorecard. It takes you through seven major financial indicators with your business and you self-score. The goal is to get a sense of how your business is doing. It may be time to raise your hand and admit that you may need some help.

It goes over things from pricing, how you do your pricing, how you pay your bills, how you collect money, how much do you have in the bank, etc. I invite people to access it and you can choose to be honest with yourself or not, but it is a great assessment to start with.

Grab your gift from Anne Dickinson at: www.SuperwomanBook.com/gifts

## My Advice for You in Your Journey

From my perspective, if you've started a business or you're running a business and you're doing it by the seat of your pants, I would encourage you to run it from a point of confidence and knowledge. It will definitely lower your stress level. If you have employees, it'll lower everyone's stress level, which only leads to peace, prosperity, and playfulness.

It's empowering to raise your hand and say, "You know, I don't get it". That's okay. You just have to be willing to get the help. It's a partnership to get the support you need to help you understand and move forward.

Run your business from a point of confidence and knowledge. It will lower your stress level.

~ Anne Dickinson

# AMPLIFYING THE VOICES OF BLACK, INDIGENOUS, WOMEN OF COLOR

I am heard. I am the one for this.
I got me.

*Sonali Fiske*

## My Superwoman Breakthrough

My breakthrough story was a "Do or Die" moment for me. In the span of eighty-six days, I lost my corporate job, ended a very painful relationship, had a total hysterectomy, lost my apartment, and moved in with my mom. I found myself gripping the carpet fibers in a fetal position, in complete grief and breakdown.

This was THE pivotal moment, and I was either going to die or rise. There was no middle ground.

God bless my mom. She gave me space to gestate, to go back to the comfort of home, so to speak, and be with what was recognizable and figure out my next move. After weeks of having regressed back to this almost fetal state, the rise, came quietly. I unearthed a long-held yearning, to attend a ten-day silent retreat. It's an ancient meditation technique called Vipassana. You shut down your phone, break off from the outside world—it's complete surrender.

As a single mother, saying goodbye to my son for that long was painful & scary. But there was no other way forward for me, I had to hush all external factors in order to dive deeper into my own self and listen to what I had to say, instead of what others wanted to hear from me.

That journey allowed me to find the work I do now—serving black indigenous, women of color, to amplify their voices, center their stories and their ancestral and traditional ways. It's still painful to travel back to this story, but that's how I found this, as my assignment here on earth.

## My Tools & Rituals to Stay in the Flow

Our rituals constantly shift. We live it as we do it. For me, a huge part of this, has been a fire of reclamation—a journey back to my own rootedness. I went back to the origins of me—before I was forced to assimilate into this dominant construct, and identify with how this oppressive system sees me. I had to look harder at the ancestors from whom I came, that meant honoring the matriarchs—my grandmother, my mother and the forced choices they had to take—and gave homage to them. I also felt a fire to be unapologetic about my greatness, be real and return to my spirituality.

I'm not a practicing Buddhist. I'm not affiliated with any specific religion, but I trust that the spiritual ways and traditions that were handed down through the generations are there for our wholeness.

My meditation practice has been an incredibly grounding, powerful way to honor and be who I am. I've been practicing for about sixteen years now. There's no way I could be a solopreneur, show up on social media, be a single mom, a leader, speaker, and all those iterations, without having that practice to ground me, calm me, and root me.

## My Purpose Is

There are so many black and brown women who come from marginalized communities and intersectional identities, incredible, teachers, mentors, writers, healers, and activists. They are speaking up and sharing their rituals, practices, healing modalities, and teachings. In fact, they are often being spoken of and about. They are often called the "voiceless." I call BS on this whole narrative. They are being who they are, but they're not always being heard.

It's my conviction and joy to amplify those voices, those of my melanated sisters. It's time black, indigenous, women of color (BIWOC) take up more intentional space in the mainstream, in industry, in our communities, online, at conferences and on the stage, as they speak up for the causes and issues they care about.

These women are our culture shifters. Our way showers. Our truth tellers. They embody so much rich traditional knowledge & indigenous wisdom, that informs the emerging narrative. So my passion is centering those voices and helping them stand in their power and their presence.

Right now, my program, "Raise Your Voice 2020," teaches BIWOC how to stand in their fire & their unapologetic truth, give TEDx talks, keynotes, give kick-ass TV/radio interviews, and how to pitch themselves with clarity and confidence. It's time for this. Past time.

## My Gift for You

My gift is a powerful talk called "From Cultural Appropriation to Reclaiming and Healing Wounds of Colonization".

Grab your gift from Sonali Fiske at: www.SuperwomanBook.com/gifts

## My Advice for You in Your Journey

So many women hang on and wait their turn, and I get it. I used to be the kind of coach that would say, "Take the lead. You need to get out of your comfort zone." But I recognize that there's a safety factor that must be considered.

Take your time. If you're not ready to jump, then listen to that inner knowing. Trust your inner guidance system, built into you by your ancestors. You will know. Recognize that you may need to marinate in that space a little bit. But at some point, you will want to take the leap. And when you do, trust that your ancestors have your back, they are with you, rooting you on every step of the way!

When you're ready, you don't have to do it alone. Do it with a loving, gentle nurturer—somebody holding your hand. That's what I do for you. I got you. I work with this feeling of loneliness and isolation. You're not alone. You have a loving, nurturing sisterhood holding you and guiding you. So when you need that, reach out. Let people know how they can support you. That's important.

Take your time. If you're
not ready to jump, then
listen to that inner
knowing. Trust your inner
guidance system, built into
you by your ancestors.

~ Sonali Fiske

# MY YEAR OF CRAZY
I am empowered and on-purpose.

*Carol Ann DeSimine*

## My Superwoman Breakthrough

I call 2015 My Year of Crazy. It was a year of breakdowns before my next big breakthrough.

I started out as an entrepreneur in 2006, doing one-on-one graphic design, photography, and publishing, in a creative services agency. I had plenty of clients and was quite successful, even surviving a significant economic downturn. But I got burned out by the one-on-one work. I'd also hit a financial glass ceiling.

In 2012, I attended my first eWomen's Network meeting. It felt like the speaker was talking directly to me, so I plucked out my money and hired her on the spot. I'd never even heard of coaching before and didn't have any desire to invest in myself in that way. But the next thing I knew, I was in her high-end mastermind. I went all in.

This mentor talked about leverage. That was the first time I had heard the term, and I knew that I wanted to leverage my worth. So I created my first signature system, the Sizzle System of Personal Branding. I still had one-on-one clients—some of whom were phasing out, and some who kept me going financially.

I put myself out there online and launched the Sizzle System group program in 2014. It was fairly successful, but some of my off-line clients saw my new online business, and they didn't like what I was doing. I guessed that they didn't understand it and perceived that it was taking away from the work I was doing for them. One situation got pretty nasty, and I had to leave that client relationship altogether. Another was even crazier and totally blindsided me. When you hear the term, "Haters gonna hate," that's how I felt for the first time in my life.

While I was dealing with these situations, I also attracted other smaller difficulties. A lawyer went wacko on me out of the blue. A summer storm devastated my neighborhood. I was the victim of a scam. I fell for it because I was so vulnerable with all the other chaos going on. I launched The Sizzle System again during that time, but even my webinar broke down. I hit one setback after another.

Most of what I tried felt like such a struggle, and I had this constant gnawing in the pit of my stomach. I knew I was just going through the motions, and for the first time I felt that I wasn't living my purpose. As someone who believes in the Law of Attraction, I tried shifting my mindset out of fear, but things seemed to get crazier and crazier. I attracted new coaching clients, but a few turned out to be crazy situations in their own right.

In the midst of it, my father's journey with Alzheimer's progressed quickly and he passed in October of that year.

In the last days of Dad's life, I had to step up as a leader in my family, a role that I had been resisting most of my life. I was older than my five brothers, but I didn't want the responsibility that came with being the oldest of six children—and the only girl.

Dad's passing was the turning point where I realized that all these crazy events were merely things falling away out of my life to clear the way for something bigger. They were messages for me to "wake up," as the Universe course-corrected my path. I firmly believe that.

As I mourned my father's passing, I felt an empowerment that wasn't there before. I declared, "This craziness is going to end NOW. I'm moving forward." I picked myself up and set out on a journey to discover my higher purpose. I owned my role as a leader. Things opened up. I started enrolling better-fit clients and earning more money. I hosted a workshop, and it was magical. I know Dad was with me that day.

I had read the book, The Big Leap, and I realized that I was working in my Zone of Excellence when I needed to step into my Zone of Genius. I was doing branding work at the time, but I started attracting clients who were less interested in branding and more interested in discovering their higher purpose. So I started helping them to find their purpose, as I was on the same journey for myself. It felt very woo woo and indecisive at times, so I developed a system around it where I traced back my life path and revealed what I was meant to do.

I sought out several healers, and they all said the same thing: "Carol Ann, you have to teach others what you went through. You have so much wisdom. This is your true purpose."

It was a mindset shift to accept that I could create a business around empowering others, rather than delivering something tangible. After the year of crazy came a year of releasing. I put my trust in the universe. I hosted a virtual summit about overcoming fear and recognizing the abundance around us. Every time I wondered how I was going to keep my business afloat, I signed on another client. But even though the money came in, it didn't look like I wanted it to.

Once I started moving toward what I felt was my higher purpose, however, things started opening up even more. I was much happier. I decided to "reset to zero." I reevaluated what wasn't working for me anymore, both inside and outside of my business.

I evolved away from the branding work. My passion was to help women play a bigger game, and I had to do so as well. I was ready, but I had to take a few steps back before I could move forward. I did more soul searching, and I channeled my new brand, Align Believe Create. I got back to teaching yoga and held women's retreats at my home. I created a new program, Goddess Unleashed, to empower women to play full out and fully expressed. Clients started asking me to help them write their book and I came up with a program to do that, too. I had finally found my true passion.

## My Tools & Rituals to Stay in the Flow

I had to utilize a lot of tools, especially when life was at its craziest. I had my chakras balanced. I practiced yoga almost every day. I worked with healers, and even ended up getting certified in I.E.T. because I felt called to work with the angels. Now I work with a healer who clears my energy every two weeks. I meditate, journal, and connect with spirit daily. I receive messages that reassure me that things are going to be okay.

## My Purpose Is

I help women unleash their inner goddess to play full out and fully expressed. We are only on this earth, in this iteration, once. Take advantage of it. I mentor them one-on-one to make a bigger impact.

In Goddess Unleashed I teach my Align Believe Create process. When you align your business with your soul's purpose, you can create success with so much more ease. I learned the hard way that when you're not aligned, everything seems hard because you don't believe in it whole-heartedly. So, believe is the second step in my process, and that's about mindset. Once you learn the strategies, mindset becomes more important because you will be faced with challenges along the way. Create is the third step of the process. I love to help women get really clear on the value and the outcome of their programs, books, and other offers.

## My Gift for You

My gift is Monetize Your Brilliance, a workbook and audio training that helps women get clear on their purpose and guides them through a process to assess their core values, gifts and talents, and craft their Soul's Calling Story.

Grab your gift from Carol Ann DeSimine at: www.SuperwomanBook.com/gifts

## My Advice for You in Your Journey

I have three pieces of advice to share.

When I was going through my Year of Crazy, my theme for the year was "boundaries." I tolerated a lot that I shouldn't have because I was in such a vulnerable place. I didn't want to put up with that anymore, and setting boundaries helped me to take my power back.

My first piece of advice is to have your boundaries. Know when to say no, but also when to say yes. Abundance, money, and whatever you desire usually come in the way of opportunities first. Don't be afraid to say yes.

The second piece of advice is to work on loving yourself. That can be hard to do, especially for women, since we tend to put ourselves last.

The third is to go after your purpose. Find out what it is. You might know, deep down in your heart, and you might be denying it. Get it out into the world. Live it. Remember, your purpose isn't about you. It's about what you do for others. By expressing your purpose, you're making the world a better place overall.

Oprah Winfrey says, "Turn your wounds into wisdom." Our life lessons can be our greatest teacher, and our greatest gift to others.

Go after your purpose.
Find out what it is. Get
it out into the world.
Live it.

~ Carol Ann Desimine

# WHEN LIFE TAKES YOUR MOM, YOU HELP MAKE MOMMIES
## And Do Some Bomb Ass Research Along the Way!

*Dr. Cleopatra Kamperveen*

## My Superwoman Breakthrough

When I tell people that I help women prepare for and get pregnant by capitalizing on the period of time leading up to pregnancy—what I call the primemester™—the first question they ask is how I got into this type of work.

I answer honestly. I tell them that my work chose me. My mother died when my twin sister and I were born. She was twenty-seven years old. By purely physiological reproductive standards, that is not too old or too young; it's just right, actually. But, I think that we would all agree that she was much too young to die.

My mother's passing was, to say the least, a very rocky start to life. But it was also a profoundly impactful start to my life that directed me to my purpose very early in life. I didn't need to know the scientific literature to know that it's nearly impossible to be healthy in the absence of a healthy mom (or a mom, period); I got the message loud and clear from Day One. I was living it, and I was struggling like crazy to defy the odds—mentally, physically, financially, and otherwise.

At a young age, I became fascinated with moms and women who would one day become moms. I observed them very closely. I wanted to understand why moms often looked unhappy and stressed. What would make life better for them? What did they need? Why did it seem like they rarely asked for help? And, to me, the most intriguing question of all: What was different about the women who seemed to effortlessly flow through what I now call the Mommy Lifecycle—specifically, conceiving, pregnancy, childbirth, parenting, and life in general?

Even as a little girl, I had a burning need to know these things.

I developed a love of writing, especially about these questions. I started college at the University of Miami one month after my eighteenth birthday. This blows my mind when I think of it now, but I had never even heard of research when I entered college! (I was constantly researching and studying health-related topics as an adolescent; but, somehow, I had never heard of, or been talked to about, the formal research enterprise. It seems crazy to me that this is even possible, but it's true.) That same month I started college, I learned about research and immediately began doing scientific research on reproductive health in a lab.

It changed my world. All those questions I had, I now had a way to answer them beyond just thinking about them and making informal observations. I never looked back.

I was hungry for knowledge, and I was hungry to make a difference for women and their children with that knowledge. I couldn't stop. I went on to do a PhD at UCLA in health and social psychology and statistics. I went on and on. I did postdoctoral training at the University of Michigan in social epidemiology, population health, and human development. From there, at age thirty-one, I started my faculty position at the University of Southern California, where I just got tenure.

For me to have somehow made the journey through so much amazing education and training; to have helped to make a difference in the lives of the hundreds of women and families I have had the great privilege and honor of helping and supporting in their pregnancy prep and conceiving process; and to be a tenured professor at USC is nothing short of a miracle. On top of that, I was the first woman of color in history to be hired on the tenure-track in the USC Davis School of Gerontology, where I started my faculty position and maintain a secondary appointment today.

My parents came to the United States a few years before I was born. They had nothing. My mom died because we had nothing. My mother's death was entirely preventable, but she died because she didn't receive even the basic standard of medical care. That was 1978, but, sadly, the same factors that contributed to my mother's death still happen in the world today.

The US healthcare system puts women of color and their children at tremendous risk during pregnancy, childbirth, and the postpartum period. This is often the result of biases that doctors, nurses, and other medical staff don't even realize they have and usually don't mean to have. It is not that this is happening on purpose, generally-speaking. But that doesn't change that it can have unspeakable consequences, as it did for my family.

Through my body of scientific research, my personal searching, and all of the observations I make day in and day out, I realized that the key to making the world a healthier, happier, more loving and supportive place for women and their children is to focus in on the primemester. It's like Pareto's Law or the Butterfly Effect, where one small shift can make all the difference in the world.

The primemester represents a critical window of opportunity, where everything that you hope will come after it—conceiving with ease, staying pregnant, carrying a pregnancy to term, having a healthy baby, and having a healthy, happy family and future—becomes that much more possible.

What no one ever tells us is that our reproductive health is so much bigger than us.

I want every woman and girl in the world to have the advantage of knowing about the primemester and how to capitalize on its power and magic. By using science-based, big-hearted tools during the primemester, we can create a domino effect of beautiful health and well-being that benefits not only us as individuals, but also our children, and grandchildren, and the entire planet.

At our core, that's what all of us want. That is the shared value of almost every human, everywhere in the world, who wants to have children. Families are the building blocks of every society, and girls and women provide the foundation for those building blocks; they are the very source of those building blocks.

It turns out that I am obsessed with the uterus. In my office, I have this beautiful uterus painting from a talented artist in the UK named Emma Plunkett. As someone who helps people prepare for and get pregnant, I am of course obsessed with the function of the uterus. But, as an activist, I am also obsessed with what the uterus represents. The uterus of a woman or girl is one of the most precious and valuable human resources available on the planet.

That precious human resource can be a gateway to generations of hardship and suffering. Or it can be a gateway to a level of progress and expansion that continues on for generations. The latter is the portal that we want our uterus to be for ourselves, our children and grandchildren, our great grandchildren, and for the planet we all share.

I developed the term primemester because I know how important it is for that domino effect to take place. I want to make sure that the primemester becomes a household word. I want every woman to understand the power they possess to shape their biological clock, their fertility, their conceiving and pregnancy experiences, what it's like to be a mom, and their future family. I want women all over the world to claim their self-authority when it comes to their reproductive health, their reproductive power, and their reproductive potential.

My beginning was so difficult because my mother didn't have this power.

Even though my start to life was super challenging, I have been determined to use it to help make healthy, happy moms all over the world. I have dedicated my life to this mission.

I can't tell you what it feels like to celebrate all of the healthy moms and healthy babies I have been so privileged to help women and couples receive. Don't be surprised if you see me jumping up and down, squealing with the biggest grin on my face and happy tears in my eyes. It's just me celebrating another positive pregnancy test, ultrasound photo, or birth announcement. It is one of the most amazing things that I could do in the world through my scholarship, my research, my writing, my direct work with women, and my support of the healthcare providers who work with women.

This year, I received the most amazing gift. For the first time ever (to my knowledge), I had a birthday baby! One of my clients gave birth to their baby on my birthday! It was, and is, truly magical for me. Knowing that I share a birthday with a baby I worked so hard to help her parents receive is something that I will cherish for the rest of my life. I actually get to visit her soon, and I am ridiculously excited.

## My Tools & Rituals to Stay in the Flow

I am all about doing life fully awake, eyes open, really seeing what is there. The more you enter into the most important decisions and parts of your life consciously and deliberately—

with intentionality—the more likely you are to end up where you want to be. If you don't know where you want to go, then you're a lot less likely to get there.

The same is true of your fertility, your biological clock, and your ability to have a healthy pregnancy and the family that you've been dreaming about for as long as you can remember. The first step is to get clear about how you want your family and your life to look.

It doesn't mean we can control everything, nor do we want to try. It just means that we get to be proactive about who we want to be and the life we want to live, rather than merely reacting to whatever comes our way. It means not defaulting into decisions—like missing out on having children—by passively letting life and time make decisions for us.

Often, women come to me uncertain about whether they want to have children. In cases like these, it's a process of, first, doing some excavating to figure out if they want to be a mom. If they decide that they do, the next task is to figure out the ideal timing of motherhood based on their goals, desires, financial situation, and also their biological clock.

However, there's another layer beneath the surface that I observe very frequently: It's what I call, being on the fence of their lives or their relationship more specifically. What I mean by being on the fence of their relationship is second-guessing the partner they chose and the life they have made together. When we second-guess, it's impossible to go all in. And love and family—and even fertility—really require us to go all in.

The women I work with often express doubt about whether they'll be on the same page as their partner when it comes to parenting, whether they'll enjoy parenting with that person, or whether there will be a lot of friction because they have differing opinions or values. They wonder if they truly want to be 'stuck' with that person for the rest of their lives. If they are having trouble getting or staying pregnant, they wonder if it is a sign that they aren't supposed to be with that person.

Having children with someone can be such a magical experience. It can also be incredibly difficult if you do it with someone who doesn't take you as you are; someone whose love and acceptance feel conditional; someone who's critical; someone who's quick to push your buttons or has the impulse to hurt you when you're vulnerable; or even someone with whom you quite simply just can't seem to live in peace. Drama doesn't make us feel safe, and our bodies are not as open to receiving and maintaining a pregnancy when we don't feel safe. Bottom line. It is a natural part of our evolutionary biology.

It's not hard to imagine how concerns and questions like these can be roadblocks to robust fertility.

The solution is to get clarity on questions like these. Be deliberate and intentional about how, with whom, and the timing in which you create your family. Know that you have way more influence over your biological clock, your fertility, and your pregnancy and mothering experiences than anyone ever tells you. Be intentional about it.

## My Purpose Is

I am Executive Director of the Fertility & Pregnancy Institute (FPI), where we use the Dr. Cleopatra Protocol to assist and support three unique but related audience segments in service of women's reproductive health and the transmission of good mental and physical health across generations.

These three audience segments include, of course, women and couples who want an evidence-based, highly successful system for preparing pregnancy and getting pregnant. We also have a certificate program for health professionals who want to integrate the Dr. Cleopatra Protocol into their work with patients and clients so that they have a highly effective system for helping them with fertility and pregnancy.

Finally, we work with the healthcare sector to support health insurance companies, fertility specialists, and other types of providers in their support of women and couples in creating their families.

Importantly, the things that we do during the primemester to prepare for pregnancy are the very same things we must do to preserve and extend our fertility for as long as possible, to prepare for egg freezing, and to maximize odds of successful IVF or other type of intervention.

For precisely this reason, we license the Protocol to fertility specialists and other healthcare providers, so that they can make it available to their patients to layer on top of the medical intervention patients are there to receive, but also to increase the success rates of the specialists and facilities themselves. The research clearly demonstrates that there are modifiable (i.e., changeable) individual difference factors that make people more or less likely to succeed in IVF or other assistive reproductive technologies. It is generally not within the scope of work of the fertility clinics to address each of these modifiable factors, so, instead, they outsource it to us. It's a beautiful win-win, benefitting both the patients and the clinic or facility as a whole.

The FPI Dr. Cleopatra Protocol—which is truly the world's best pregnancy preparation and conceiving protocol (and not just because I'm biased!)—takes a systems approach to fertility. If you can picture the neural network in the brain, or a cell phone network, or an electricity grid: Fertility is the same. It is a network, a system, a constellation. It is not just in the hormones, or in the vagina, or in the cervix, or in the uterus, or in the fallopian tubes. It is throughout the body, it is in the mind, it is in the heart, it is in the bedroom, it is in the kitchen, it is in the office, it is in the history, and it is in the identity. It is also in the atmosphere: In the physical environment, the surrounding support structures, and the cultural context. Healthy fertility, healthy pregnancies, and healthy babies depend on all of these things in concert and in how they interact with our DNA.

That is the truth of what determines fertility.

The Dr. Cleopatra Protocol capitalizes on the power in the primemester to systematically address the psychological, biological, neural (or brain-related), social, and cultural factors that affect the biological clock, fertility, and conceiving.

When we do this, women and couples are more likely to conceive quickly and easily, to reduce risk of miscarriage and other complications, and to have a healthy baby and a graceful, calm transition to parenthood.

The preparation we do is not just physiological; it is psychological, cognitive, social, relational, and cultural as well. The Dr. Cleopatra Protocol uses the science of epigenetics (or gene expression), intricate psychology-fertility feedback loops, and scientifically validated mind-body practices to guide women and couples through a step-by-step blueprint for preserving, extending, and amplifying their fertility so that they can have a baby easily, now or ten years from now.

What's interesting is that the form of preparation that we do in the Dr. Cleopatra Protocol doesn't apply just to the people who provide the DNA for the baby. It is critical for everyone who will provide the container in which the process of conceiving, pregnancy, and child development will take place.

Pregnancy preparation and the work of the primemester is the work of moms and dads in every possible type of partnership, including heterosexual, LGBTQIA, and everything else that we have concrete language for today and are certain to have concrete language for in the future. It is the work of both biological and social parents.

In 2018, our 12-month success rate was 97%. That success rate is remarkable under any circumstance; but it is especially remarkable when you understand that the vast majority of people who come to work with us have struggled to get pregnant for months, years, or even a decade. The Protocol is incredibly powerful. The combination of scientific training and tools, community, accountability, and support is incredibly powerful. I am so proud of it, and I am so proud of what it does for women and their families. Because of it, there is purpose in the rocky start to my life. Because of the Protocol and the way it changes lives, nothing is wasted. I am overflowing with appreciation.

We collect a lot of data, of course—I am a scientist after all! We're mainly concerned with whether or not people get pregnant and how long it takes. But, in addition to that, we see huge improvements—ranging from 83% to 100%—in areas such as physical health, mental health, reproductive health, romantic relationship, self-esteem, and professional life.

When I initially conceived of this work twenty-three years ago, my intention was that every woman in the world who knows that she wants to have babies, whether in the near or distant future, would do this preparation and learn how to capitalize fully on the magic and the power of the primemester.

My dream is to create an educational revolution where the primemester is a household word and where everyone does this preparation, just as they would prepare for the SAT, a job interview, a marathon, or their wedding day. The health of our fertility and our babies is actually far more consequential than any of these things. Yet, for some reason, we spend far more time preparing for everything else. Doesn't that blow your mind (and not in a good way) when you think about it! We have this strange idea that because getting pregnant is 'natural', it will happen easily and doesn't require preparation or even much attention.

That is not true. Getting pregnant, in reality, is not nearly as easy as we are made to believe as adolescents and teenagers. And making the most out of our fertility and our families requires energy, effort, and attention, just like making the most out of our education and our physical fitness does.


## My Gift for You

I have a beautiful, sassy, fun, and tremendously effective mini-course called, Your Fertility Unleashed: The Pleasure Portal to Your Fertility, where you will learn things about your fertility that you never knew! Hint. One of the things you will learn is how to use pleasure (and, yes, this includes physical pleasure!) during the primemester to conceive quickly and easily.

Grab your gift from Dr. Cleopatra Kamperveen at: www.SuperwomanBook.com/gifts

## My Advice for You in Your Journey

One of the most important lessons that I have ever learned came to me through my faculty position. The lesson is this. People will say things about you. They will tell you what is and isn't possible for you. This includes people who are powerful, smart, and widely respected and influential. But none of that matters. The only thing that matters is that you know that the things people say about you, including about what is or isn't possible for you, are only true if you believe them.

Don't let anyone's limited vision of you limit this one life you have. Shine on, beauty!

If you believe yourself
worthy of the thing you
fought so hard to get,
then you help the soul of
the world and you
understand why you are
here.

~ Paulo Coelho

# THE BREAKDOWN BEFORE
# THE BREAKTHOUGH
I am responsible for my own
happiness.

*Kathy Murray*

## My Superwoman Breakthrough

My breakthrough started when I left my twenty-five-year career as a CFO for a private school to become an entrepreneur. I didn't know the first thing about it because I was a corporate career woman.

At the time, I was a rather unhappy wife. Thankfully, I found an incredible author and fell in love with her work. I became passionate about empowering other women to become happy wives. I left my corporate job to help her build this business to reach women and end divorce throughout the world. Five years later, I'd helped hundreds of thousands of women and built a million-dollar company that required my attention 24/7.

Or so I thought.

In the fall of 2018, we were on track to reach that million-dollar mark for the first time. I was running it mostly by myself. I was frustrated and overwhelmed. But I didn't want anyone to know. I wanted to hide my fears and my concerns. I feared my family's response when I said, "I can't do things with you. I'm too busy. I have an interview. I have a meeting or a class."

I was largely unaware of the level of burnout I'd reached. But I found myself in the emergency room on the Saturday before Thanksgiving. I realized that I'd been ignoring my body while trying to grow this company from zero to a million in five years.

And the sad news is that I teach this stuff! Self-care is one of the indispensable first steps in my program. I'm passionate about teaching women to take care of themselves first, like putting on their own oxygen before they help their children. And yet, when it came to building this company to help women and save marriages, I forgot my own work. My own self-care was not at the level that is required to run $1 million company, let alone to reach my vision of building it to ten times that volume.

That ER visit led to a pretty scary diagnosis, and ultimately to surgery in January and six months of chemotherapy.

I had no idea what kind of transformation and growth was in store for me in regard to self-care, vulnerability, and letting go. I was filled with a lot of fear. But I had to let go and take care of myself at that point. I had no other choice!

So many people rallied around me. People came out of the woodwork offering help. I really grew in my capacity for receiving, relinquishing control, and being vulnerable. As a result, I was able to focus entirely on my well-being during that time.

So, surprisingly, not only did other leaders emerge in my company, but my plate emptied. After the surgery, when I started to feel better and to do some of the work again, I decided to not refill the plate as full as it has been. My default mode was busy, busy, busy, do, do, do. But I wanted to just be. I gained a lot of insight about how I could produce the same results by standing for other people's greatness rather than always having to be the one to do it.

The most important lesson I learned out of this ordeal was practicing self-care at a whole new level without guilt, and without fear that my business partner, Laura, would doubt my capacity during this time. I focused on becoming my best self, and I had the most successful six months in the whole five years of my business. I sold more in the last six months than I did in those previous years, because I didn't overfill my plate. I focused on my passion, which is connecting deeply with other women and standing for their vision and their desire to either become a coach with us or to save their marriage and become a happy wife.

There are so many hurting women and I want to serve them. But I realize now that I don't have to work so hard to be successful. Sometimes it just takes getting out of the way to find the right team and the structures to support the thousands of women who need help. I can stand in a vision and praise and acknowledge other people. I can seek out support and let go.

And I'm so grateful, now, for that health crisis because I don't think I would have learned those lessons any other way. As painful and as scary as that incident was—the diagnosis, the treatment, all of it—it was a blessing. Now I play on weekends. I don't work on the weekends; I close my laptop. That was unheard of before.

## My Tools & Rituals to Stay in the Flow

I walk in the mornings now. I take time for meditation and journaling. I take weekends off.

I make time for fun and creativity. I just spent a weekend by myself on a silent retreat in a beautiful little resort. I'm writing a book. I travel to see some girlfriends. A friend of mine asked me if I want to paint. I'm not sure, but I figured, "What the heck. Let's try it." I'm going to be sixty this year, and I decided that I want to do something really fun. So I'm going hot-air ballooning with my daughters.

## My Purpose Is

We help women become happy wives and become their best selves where they feel desired, cherished, and adored every single day in her marriage.

Women frequently ask me for advice or tips. I always tell them to get a guide. Get a coach. You need a roadmap, a pathway.

I know I couldn't have done it without my marriage mentor. They don't teach you about marriage in school. There are no classes on how to be a happy wife or how to foster good relationships. So get a guide. Be open to uncovering your blind spots and experimenting with techniques that may be counterintuitive or out of the box.

I tried the old standards, like dragging him to marriage counseling. It never worked. And the women I speak to say the same thing. So I invite women to get a roadmap.

## My Gift for You

My gift is called the Adored Wife Roadmap. It shows you the steps to take to have an intimate, passionate, and peaceful relationship. Those steps lead you to becoming a dignified woman full of peace and intimacy who attracts prosperity. You'll find that once all of the arguing stops, a lot more prosperity comes to your door. It impacts every area of your life.

But your marriage doesn't have to be broken to benefit from the Adored Wife Roadmap. Even in a healthy marriage, The Adored Wife Roadmap will lead to deeper intimacy and make your relationship better.

Grab your gift from Kathy Murray at:
www.SuperwomanBook.com/gifts

## My Advice for You in Your Journey

Say yes to yourself. Take a moment to ask yourself what
you want and how you feel. Then find the right mentor, the
right guide, and the right roadmap to get you there.

Take a moment to ask
yourself what you want
and how you feel.

~ Kathy Murray

# I AM THE MASTERPIECE
# WHO MASTERS PEACE

*Liana Chaouli*

## My Superwoman Breakthrough

My breakthrough moment happened as I took care of a client many years ago. She was powerful and consciously congruent to who she was in all the domains of her life – as a teacher, professor, and mother to several children. But when it came to dressing, shopping, and being able to show herself to the world, she lacked mastery in applying agency to her life.

As we shopped together, I witnessed a magnificent queen brimming with self-esteem, suddenly diminish into a puddle of pain, just because a saleswoman treated her badly. This moment was similar to the famous scene with Julian Roberts in the movie Pretty Woman. In that moment I realized, "Oh my God, I will never allow this to happen to another woman again." My commitment was forged in that instant, I promised to create a path for every woman to own her authentic beauty and connect to her magnificent Self-Image.

This degrading incident reignited an old memory. I remembered dressing my mother when I was three years old. She was sick so often, unable to get herself out of her sadness and heartache. It was difficult for her to get out of bed, let alone dress herself. So I would gather all her special pieces, put them on her bed and whisper "Mommy, please get dressed. Because when you're dressed and you're beautiful you're happy, then we can go out play together."

Today almost 55 years later, my mom now tells this story on a big stage, and everyone in the room can relate. She says, "I couldn't follow my daughter's invitation, but I hope you accept her offer of support. She's the best, and believe me I know, because I was her very first client... and I know how good she is."

It's not about being a good image therapist™. It's about being a mentor, a conduit for other women to find their own "You-ness." You have got to show up as YOU because everybody else is taken.

The revelation occurred for me in the eyes and the experience of another woman. A woman who couldn't stand up for who she truly was. She could not say, "This is who I am. This is what my body looks like. I'm a figure eight. I don't need any square shoulders. I need things that are rounded. This is the kind of fabric I want and what my curves need to look amazing. You know, my booty's big enough, I don't need pockets on my booty."

I want people to find out what it's like to be empowered with who they are and how amazing they can show up. We only get this one body for our whole life. You can empower yourself to understand what your body needs. You can get a PhD in the design of who you are, no matter your age, no matter where you're going, no matter whether you're a breastfeeding mom or a CEO.

I love the look on a woman's face when she puts on an outfit I've picked for her. Something so different than what she imagines for herself, something she thinks she could never wear. Suddenly, something inside her shifts. There's a huge transformation. When I as an Image Therapist™ say, I provide transformation through the empowerment of wardrobe, I mean it. That's literally what the process of Self Image Therapy™ ™does for my clients. You learn, grow and see yourself in a whole new light. You can look at and any wardrobe item and say, "I know that when I put this on this body, it's going to be amazing, or not!"

## My Tools & Rituals to Stay in the Flow

When I feel fear, I know that I'm in resistance to something that's right in front of me. Fear has been described as False Evidence Appearing as Real. I'm most joyful when I'm in the moment with what ever is happening right here , right now , with the people who are here with me. So when fear shows up, I know that I'm not being present. I'm either in the past, or I'm in the future. But I'm not in the present moment.

At that point, my best practice is to get back into my body. Our Bodies are the placeholder for all things, everything happens in our vessel. Most people live ten feet away from their bodies. But my work, which is all about embodiment, is a path to bringing you back into this body, and into this moment. Right now, in this moment, I have a roof over my head. I'm healthy. I have a beautiful table to sit at. I have food in my fridge. So when you narrow it down, the fear is out there … not here.

But when you look at all the blessings in front of you, all these beautiful, amazing, minute wonders – you know, moments of magic – there's nothing to fear. There's nothing there but wonder and gratitude.

To be embodied in this moment, feel the insides of your eyelids. Because life only happens in this moment. Life doesn't happen in the past and it doesn't happen in the future. It's happening now… and now… and now!

# My Purpose Is

First, together we explore and uncover your "You-ness." I take you from the bud that you are to the blossom that you have the capacity to become. Wherever you go, there you are. And usually, your clothes are with you because we don't go anywhere naked. They are your second skin, and as important as your first skin.

I's been clear to me since I was a young girl, that our clothing and the relationship we have to it (which I call your second skin) has a huge impact on our Being, the way we behave and how we interact with the world. When we are stuck in the past, and we don't really see ourselves for who we are, we have a hard time expressing the beauty of who we are with our clothes. Then clothing becomes the armor to shield the shame, rather than the frame which shows off our magnificence.

But I want to take you from shame to shining. Let's unveil your spirit so we can dress the masterpiece that your body is. And I do that through a process of Self Image Therapy ™, through giving you an understanding of what your body needs – your body; not your sister's, not your mother's.

There's a structure, a system by which you can learn what your body needs, what kind of architecture, which shapes are most flattering and why certain colors and fabric make you shine. An Oak tree never wants to be an orchid and vice versa. But we humans tend to say, "I wish I was skinnier. I wish I had bigger boob, a smaller butt, I wish I was... this or that."

But my system stays within the moment! What's in front of you in the mirror – twenty pounds less or more, size two or size twenty-two – doesn't matter. The system and it's principals can be applied to anything, no matter where you are, or where you go.

The process of Self Image Therapy ™is a designed system that teaches you how to look amazing, no matter your size, shape, color or height. You learn what colors look great on you, what should stay in your closet and what should leave, why you can wear certain prints and not others. It's a systematic way to understand what to buy and what to avoid. It will empower you for the rest of your life.

You don't go by what the fashion industry dictates, because that's not important. I don't care if you bought it at Target or Neiman Marcus. It has got to look amazing on YOU. You are the masterpiece and everything else has to beautifully uphold and embolden this masterpiece. Clothes have to frame YOUR MASTERPIECE.

## My Gift for You

My gift is a video series that teaches you the foundational work of image therapy™ so you can take immediate action. It's so powerful to receive the feedback we receive from our clients after they've had a chance to watch, learn and implement "Oh my God,I learned so much. I'm so excited to put it all into action" Yes, there is much to learn. I've been doing this work for thirty years, and it's like math. You start with the foundation of, "One plus one is two," and then "Two times two is four." Then you go to Algebra. But first you start with the foundation.

Grab your gift from Liana Chaouli at: www.SuperwomanBook.com/gifts

## My Advice for You in Your Journey

I believe I am the masterpiece who masters peace. I say that because I believe that peace does not start on the borders of our country, but inside of me. When I am at peace with who I truly am, where I am, who I love, what I love, and who's in my life, I can be the beacon of peace for another.

When I have no resistance, I can be the light of someone else's peace. YOU can take you candle, your bright light, and can give it to someone else. They can say, "I want what she's got." Or, "If she has it, I can have it." When I am at peace with myself, I can give that gift to someone else.

That's the basis of prosperity. It's not money. It's not the size of our bank account. It's not how much someone is paying me. It's being at peace with myself, so I can be a light onto the world, for someone else to come and light their candle on mine.

Because you your light can light a billion other candles without ever diminishing its own source

The beauty of a woman
must be seen from in her
eyes, because that is the
doorway to her heart, the
place where love resides.

~ Audrey Hepburn

# CREATING MY FREEDOM IN BUSINESS & LIFE
I am in charge of my life. I am free.

*Tye Miles*

## My Superwoman Breakthrough

My breakthrough moment was both scary and exhilarating.

I have fifteen years in the beauty industry. I've built from scratch a seven-figure company around styling hair and owning a salon. However, I got to a point in my business where every extra dollar meant extra wear and tear on my body. I developed carpal tunnel.

I had no time for my family. I had created this financial success, but I wasn't part of the picture. Literally, there were days where I sent my family on vacation without me. It was no longer fulfilling for me. My drive was gone; I was unmotivated.

Earlier in my business, I got very excited about some new aspect of it. I'd read everything I could, go to conferences, and learn everything there was to know about the most current thing.

I stopped doing all of that because I wasn't as excited anymore. That really disheartened me.

So, I reached this place in my life where I needed to know how I could scale my business successfully so that I could have time freedom—so that I could enjoy the vacations, the baseball games, the volleyball games, and the basketball games with my family.

Could I do that in a way that I could regain that zest for what I was so passionate about?

I realized that I could not. Something bigger, something greater was pulling at me, calling me forward, and I decided to do that new thing. That meant completely shifting industries. I was afraid of what other people would think about me going from a beautician to a coach, a consultant, and a speaker.

Would people take me seriously? How would this look for my credibility as I tried to build this new thing? At the end of the day, I decided that I only get one life, and I refused to live with regrets.

So I decided, "Hey, I'm going to do it!" Now, this was really risky for me, for my household. I was the biggest earner in my household. I historically earned more money than my husband. My kids were used to a certain lifestyle.

A lot was on me, not only from my personal family, but I had other stylists in my salon. Their livelihoods were based upon the business that I was trying to get out of. Their families depended on this business. My clients depended on us—high profile clients from all around the city, and even flying in to see me. They'd be affected by this change, too.

I had all this weighing on me—everybody's expectations. What it would be like? How would it be different?

So I basically decided, "You only get to live once. Let's see the best way to adjust and transition from this."

And so I did it.

Now, this huge transition from one industry to a completely new industry taught me that, more than anything, you have to learn how to trust your intuition. I had to trust that divine discontent, that unhappiness, that loss of motivation that I felt from the beauty industry. I had to invite something new into my life and lean into that invitation.

I had to learn how to trust my intuition. I had to learn how to trust my own power to make a decision for myself—not for my husband, not for my family, not for the stylists, not for my clients. I had to own that decision and what that would look like for me.

I also had to learn how to trust other people, because I was doing something totally new that I knew nothing about. I had to trust that other people could use their brilliance to cover my blind spots so that my baby, this new business vision, could come forth.

So I'm very excited. We're almost three years into this thing, and I'm so happy that I made the transition.

## My Tools & Rituals to Stay in the Flow

For so long, I took myself so seriously as an overachiever. You know, as women, I think we are just highly competitive. What I wanted most was to embrace playfulness and practice patience with myself.

To do this I started a practice of daily meditation. I wake up earlier than the rest of my family so that I can have time for myself and can get that me time to center my myself and set an intention for my day. This helps inject positivity into my day and increases my productivity.

Most often, I follow that up with exercise. For me, exercise is not just to keep my body looking physically strong, but it's also about my mental health. It keeps stress low and increases my happiness level.

I also follow these guidelines called the Law of Moderation—spiritual principles of balance that I think about every day. It helps me stay true to myself. I'm at a point in my life where I've done a lot of things for a lot of other people.

I've lived up to other people's expectations. Now, I'm very protective of being sure that I show up and do me every day.

There are three principles that really stick out to me. The first Law of Moderation that I use daily is to eliminate the need to prove yourself to anyone, including yourself.

The second one is to learn that people are neither better than, nor less than you, regardless of their status or situation. It doesn't matter who they are, how much money they make, where they live, or what walk of life they come from. I am no bigger than, no better than, and no less than them.

The third one is to continually improve yourself. Neither expect too much from yourself nor too little.

These three principles are about balance. So every day, to maintain peace, playfulness, and to create that prosperous lifestyle, I'm intentional about reading at least those three things.

So many other principles—like give yourself a chance, be patient with yourself, be kind, take the time to acknowledge your wins, celebrate yourself— tie right back into that Law of Moderation, that spiritual principle of balance.

## My Purpose Is

I'm a holistic business coach. I'm a brand strategist and I'm an international speaker. Those are the titles of who I am. What I love to do is help women entrepreneurs who are ready to show up as their true selves in their businesses. I help them to discover, brand, monetize and authentically share their gifts with the world so that they can create the fulfilling lifestyle they truly desire.

## My Gift for You

My gift is Five Essentials to Create Your Own Passionately Successful Personal Brand. It's specifically for coaches, consultants, experts and entrepreneurs.

Grab your gift from Tye Miles at: www.SuperwomanBook.com/gifts

## My Advice for You in Your Journey

Own your beliefs about yourself, your life, and your decisions. Be really intentional about how you respond in life, how you show up in life, and the decisions that you make. If you do that, there is no doubt that more peace, more playfulness, and more prosperity will follow you. You'll attract it automatically.

Own your beliefs about yourself, your life, and your decisions. Be really intentional about how you respond in life, how you show up in life, and the decisions that you make.

~ Tye Miles

# THE INNER WORK TO TRANSFORM MY MONEY STORY

I am abundant and in the flow.

*Dr. Pamela Moss*

## My Superwoman Breakthrough

It was a few years ago when I really hit a low point in my business. I only had $200 in the bank and more than $1,700 in bills plus $16,000 of debt with nothing coming in.

I was so sick and tired of worrying about money! And stressing about how I was going to generate enough of it. I just wanted to run away to an ashram somewhere, where I could live a simple, holy life and help people without worrying about making a living.

I was in this really desperate situation. But then I got this message from Spirit: "Just DO YOUR INNER MONEY WORK! Stop resisting!!"

*(I had been resisting for quite awhile…)*

So I finally surrendered and spent the entire month of November doing deep inner work around money. By the end of it I knew that I had transformed my money story—the foundation of how I relate to money. And it showed! Things shifted dramatically:

The next month I made $5,000. The month after I made $14,800. And by June I'd earned more in six months than I'd made the whole previous year. I paid off my debt!

After this happened, I told my old friend and colleague Natalie Hill (a wonderful business coach) about it in a casual catch-up conversation.

Natalie said, "You should teach that process. I would take that course. My students need that course."

So I created the course, which I called "Transform Your Money Story". Natalie then invited me to launch it with her (she was my affiliate partner, and even interviewed me for the webinar) and it ended up being the most simple, easy, natural launch I've ever done—because it was totally in the flow.

What being in the flow looked like: I wrote all the launch copy (two video scripts, webinar script, email sequence, sales page) in three days, at a hotel—when usually it would take me weeks to do that. Every part of the launch worked great. It was just so aligned. Natalie and I had a blast doing the webinar together, and twenty-four perfect people came in, largely from her big list. They all got incredible results, too! Now it's a product that keeps selling, with awesome testimonials.

I learned a number of things from this experience. One of them was the importance of listening to guidance. I had been ignoring for quite a while the need to do inner work around money. I have a lot of powerful transformational tools, but I kept ignoring my intuition and just pushing through. And that wasn't working! I kept needing to learn to listen to Guidance, over and over.

Another thing that I learned was to notice where there is flow and where there is not flow. What I mean by flow is where I feel aligned and things happen easily and naturally. It's where people say "yes", and opportunities come to me without effort—that's flow. When I feel relaxed and peaceful, there's flow.

When I'm not in flow I struggle, suffer, or feel stuck. I don't tend to stay stuck because I have powerful tools, but I do get stuck sometimes like everybody else. The thing about it is there's warning signs way before the stuck place. I've finally learned to pay attention to them. I feel the warning signs in my body and start noticing tension—I carry tension in my shoulders. Or I start feeling stress, and I can't fall asleep easily or I wake up in the night. I now know that is my body is talking to me and saying, "Pamela, this isn't the right way—you're putting pressure on me!"

I've learned to pay attention to my body. I actually listen to the messages it's trying to tell me. I also pay attention to signs and patterns I notice in the world around me, in response to my intentions and actions. And I ask myself, "What's the simplest way to do this?" because my default way is to work really hard, overthink it, and be a perfectionist.

I wasn't even thinking to teach that Transform Your Money Story course, but it ended up being one of my most popular courses and very successful. It was called for (literally; she asked me to teach it) and happened so easily. I learned to listen to guidance and go with the flow—instead of what I usually do: push myself to do what think I "have to" or "should" do.

The third thing I learned is the power of strategic partnerships. My relationship with Natalie is an example of that. We've been friends for a long time, but we hadn't really done much work together. Up until then we had only done a little exchange, but we hadn't done any affiliate partnerships. Ever since then, there's a whole beautiful relationship where we deeply support each other because we have complimentary skills that serve the same people.

All three of those things were big learnings. They are reinforcements from that experience of just going down into the pit and surrendering to do the inner work that I needed to do.

## My Tools & Rituals to Stay in the Flow

I'd love to share my tools because this is what makes all the difference. It's important to have effective ways to do the inner work you need to do to shift yourself. There are three tools/processes that are my go-to foundation to make a shift and they're very, very powerful.

The first one is what I call dialoguing with trusted guidance. And that really just means a written dialogue. Like writing the lines of a play—first you write your name:

Me: "I'd like to speak to..." whatever you call your guidance. Maybe you call it 'God', or 'my heart', or 'my higher self', you ask to speak to it and listen for answers. If you don't know what your guidance is, you can just write, "I'd like to talk to my trusted guidance."

And the next thing you write is, "Are you there?"

And you write in the next line, the name of your trusted guidance, and whatever you get in response to that. It can be an emotion. It might be words, it might be a memory, just a feeling your body, whatever. Like this:

Trusted Guidance: I'm always here.

And you just go back and forth having a dialogue. It is so profoundly helpful to be able to get the higher perspective whenever you want it, by asking for it and listening for a response. It's different than prayer. Prayer is just sending it out (monologue). This is a conversation. To dialogue with your trusted guidance is super powerful and I recommend it to everybody.

The next tool is dialoguing with subconscious parts of you. This is really valuable if you're feeling stuck, fearful, angry, or uncomfortable. You can talk to that fear or discomfort. You can see what it's trying to tell you, and what it needs to give you permission to move forward, so you feel less scared.

Those two tools—dialoguing with trusted guidance and dialoguing with subconscious parts— are truly enlightening for business decisions. I use them a lot.

Then the third tool is alignment, which is something you have to learn how to do. It's basically a way of systematically replacing your fears and doubts with higher truth. Your higher truth is what's really true for you, and your true self.

Those are all very powerful ways to shift out of feeling stuck or self-sabotaging, which is something we all need to do at times. In five minutes of dialoguing with a part of you you're not consciously aware of, you can shift things in a profound way.

After you've been doing this work for a while, no matter what goes on in your life you don't go into those pits anymore. Because I've done a lot of it, I'm on an even keel in life. There are little bumps, but it's not like it was, where I could go so far up and so far down.

## My Purpose Is

Fundamentally I help people in two ways.

One is I help them get deep clarity about what they're here to do. It's not that I know that, but your system knows that. I know how to help you pull it out from deep within. What is your unique thing? What are you designed to do? What problems are you here to solve?

I love to help entrepreneurs get that clarity, because they can struggle for so long trying to figure it out. But it's actually already in existence within you. It's just pulling it out. That's one thing I love to do, help people get that deep clarity.

The second way I help people, which I also love doing, is to help them remove their obstacles or blocks to expressing who they really are, and fully being that and doing that. Those blocks are in your subconscious mind. You may feel like you're inhibited from speaking your truth, or lack confidence; you don't know why. You don't have to know why; what matters is that you can transform those blocks on a deep level, permanently and quickly.

I just want people to know that you don't have to suffer and struggle. A lot of times, when people have been stuck for years, I've been able to help them get unstuck in a very short time—by working with what they don't consciously know that they know (which is either their higher guidance or their subconscious mind.)

Those are the two core ways that I help people and my favorite things to do. It is not only life changing for them, but deeply fulfilling for me.

## My Gift for You

My gift is called the Inner Wisdom Treasure Chest. It includes thirteen incredibly powerful tools for transforming blocks and helping you gain deep clarity. I promise will change your life, because these are deep, powerful processes and it tells you when to use each one! For example, if you're in a stressful situation, there's a particular one to transform that so it's not stressful. It's very helpful. I'm happy to share my Inner Wisdom Treasure Chest with you. It's also beautiful. I had fun making it, used my artwork, and it feels like an illuminated manuscript, a book of magic.

When you sign up to get the Inner Wisdom Treasure Chest, you also can apply for the opportunity to receive a 20-minute Clarity Consult with me at no charge. The Clarity Consult is another really helpful tool if you need a boost, to see where you're stuck and what your system says you need to do to get unstuck. You will get that clarity in those 20 minutes. It's a great entree to working with me, so you can see exactly how I can help you, and I can see it too.

Grab your gift from Dr. Pamela Moss at: www.SuperwomanBook.com/gifts

## My Advice for You in Your Journey

The answers to everything you're wondering and uncertain about are inside you. And you can bring them out by asking different parts of yourself for answers, because you know so much more than you think you do. In the middle of all the chatter of self-proclaimed experts telling you "do this" or "do that," in your business or life—only you know your deep truth. That's the most important thing to tap into as an entrepreneur—you've got to shut out the noise and confusion and just follow what's resonant and authentic for you.

The answers to everything
you're wondering and
uncertain about are inside
you.

~Dr. Pamela Moss

# DESIGNING MY BUSINESS ON MY OWN TERMS

## I am honoring my flow.

*Kim Eldredge*

### My Superwoman Breakthrough

A brand-new business is, almost by definition, overwhelming! I had left my full-time position working for eleven years in my dad's tax practice, and I had given him a whole year's notice. I was so excited to get going with my business, but I only had a few clients lined up.

So on April 15th, I said, "I'm outta here!" By late June or early July of that year, I was already starting to wonder if I had made a mistake.

It wasn't so much that I was overwhelmed or disenchanted with the business itself because I loved my work' I loved helping people find their stories, share their message, and write their books. And I even had quite of bit of entrepreneurial experience!

Still, I was overwhelmed with how I managed my time and how I chased dollars. I realized that I was putting my focus in the wrong place.

One of the really instrumental moments was attending Maribel's Superwoman Entrepreneur Retreat and realizing that I didn't have to buy in to this mindset of "It's a startup. I have to run myself from pillar to post. I need to start by six in the morning, and if I end before midnight, I'm doing something wrong."

I realized that my business could feel spacious, and I could create my world the way I wanted it to be created. When I had my day job in dad's tax practice, I didn't even start my entrepreneurial workday until four, five, or six o'clock in the evening.

After quitting my day job, I tried to start my workday by 8 am. I'm a great morning person for ideas and being creative, but not for tasks like sitting down and writing for a client. Then I realized that I could start my day whenever I wanted to. So I adjusted my work hours to make time an ally. That first year of my business was all about figuring out how to design my life from that point forward.

In those early months of my business, I also felt burnt out, overwhelmed, and stressed around the money piece. I realized that I needed to get some help both on the practical side— such as how to do the bookkeeping—and on the energetic side—such as how to have fun with my business.

At the time, my business felt like a financial sprinkler— there was plenty of money, but it was shooting out from all different directions. I knew that I helped people find their message so that they could write their books, but I did it in so many different ways—little bitty coaching programs, higher-ticket programs, ghost writing, and even copy-writing.

I used the next few years in my business to explore what I really wanted to do, and how I wanted to do it. (All while supporting myself with my efforts!) And if anything started to feel too heavy or crazy-making, it went out the door.

When I became pregnant, I thought that I could still be all things to everybody after my son was born. I was not really prepared to pare down to just those services that made me happy. But I figured it out fast. Through that trial and error, I figured out what I liked, where my zone of genius was, and how I could make it a win-win for my business, my clients, and my family.

A lot of the things that I enjoyed, but were crazy-making or created overwhelm, got shuffled out of the business. I had to move things so I had more space. That shift allowed me to focus on the best ways to help my clients in a way that was most fulfilling to me—i.e., working very closely with my clients and mentoring them as they write their books.

I still love doing copywriting. When my business was new, I wrote launch copy or did ghost writing or books for anybody. Now, I do it only occasionally. I call it the dessert of my business. That boundary keeps me from getting overwhelmed.

## My Tools & Rituals to Stay in the Flow

The first ritual was making friends with time. My son will be two in September, and I have eighteen hours of childcare each week. So instead of having a battle with the clock, I focus on the tasks I get to do when the nanny is here. Shifting that mindset makes me less crazy.

My other ritual is hiking boots. I am unapologetically in love with outdoor recreation.

My husband, Ben, works out of town two to three weeks at a time, and then he's home for two weeks. At first, I limited my play to when he was home. My son and I only got out for adventures when my husband was home. I realized that it was negatively impacting my business, because I wasn't finding that time to recharge.

So now, even when Ben is out on the road, Small Thing and I figure out how to get the outdoor recreation we need. This spring, I took Small Thing camping—his second-ever camping trip—all by myself. It rained. It hailed. We slept in the back of the car. And it was such a marvelous trip because I approached it asking, "How can this be playful? How can this be fun?" We came home recharged and laughing.

## My Purpose Is

I help message driven people to finally write their books so that they can share their message. It's not a "just-add-water" type of process; there is work involved. So I break it down, step-by-step, so you can write your book and tell your stories.

I'm big on storytelling! When was the last time you remembered some acronym? And if you can remember it, when was the last time that you used the system or training it stood for?

But by teaching storytelling—especially in non-fiction book writing—you're giving the reader a gift. They feel, so they remember.

And I help you get it done!

## My Gift for You

My gift is one of the beginning pieces for how to unlock your genius so you can finally write your book. It's called The Five Mental Monsters That Keep You from Writing Your Book.

Here's the trick about the five mental monsters: there are only five. It's not like five out of a dozen. Everything that prevents you from writing your book boils down to one of these five mental monsters. So let's get them handled and get your book out there.

Grab your gift from Kim Eldredge at: www.SuperwomanBook.com/gifts

## My Advice for You in Your Journey

Your message matters. You have been given a message from God—and your purpose on the planet is to share it, to impact lives.

When you think that you don't matter, that you have nothing to say, that is' not worth the effort to shout into the void...

Share your message. Write it down, do a video, post it, create it.

Because your message matters.

Your message matters.
You have been given a
message from ~~God~~—and
your purpose on the
planet is to share it, to
impact lives.

~ Kim Eldredge

# HOW THE BUSINESS IN MY SOUL WAS BIRTHED
## I am divinely guided.

*Ronda Renee*

## My Superwoman Breakthrough

As a single mom running a business, I could pick out a million stories to share. The one that's really present for me was a situation a lot more of us are dealing with these days because we're living longer. There's a lot of us who have aging parents while we also have kids at home. They call it us the "sandwich generation."

It was six ago now, and my father was diagnosed with Multiple Myeloma, which is a cancer that's not curable. It's treatable but not curable. Unfortunately, it wasn't discovered until stage four, so it was already very advanced.

At that time, I made the choice to bring him into my home to care for him while I was also running my business and raising my kids in the same home. I work from home like so many of us do as entrepreneurs and that meant some things had to change.

There's this thing that happens when we, by necessity, have to get really efficient and effective. My father was diagnosed in January and I took on my last client for the year two weeks later and then I didn't take on another client until August. What was amazing is my business still doubled that year. That happened because I got really efficient and effective.

One of the biggest breakthroughs was the three-phase model that to this day I teach all the people that I work with in my Business In Your Soul® Program. It was birthed out of that necessity to be efficient and effective.

I was forced to get super clear on what my "lane" was. Getting crystal clear about the one thing that I do better than anybody else and committing to not do anything but my thing. That alone led to a myriad of other breakthroughs.

In the moment, it allowed me to stop trying to do anything other than the thing that is mine to do. There's a lot of things I'd love to see done in the world, but they're not all mine to do. Most of them are someone else's to do. I learned how to focus on only what I was here to do.

I didn't discover until much later that my dad would wait until Friday afternoon to tell me that he needed to go to the doctor all because he didn't want to bother me because I was working.

I can't tell you how many Friday nights I spent in the ER, because he had been holding out since Wednesday. I never told him he needed to do that. That was his own thing. This went on for about five or six months until he transitioned. It was a tough time in life to try to balance.

That whole period of my life birthed a lot of breakthroughs. The fact that my business still grew and the model that I still use to this day came out of it really shows that in every adversity, whatever you're facing, there's also this wonderful gift. There's this wonderful gem that's going to come forward and show you how strong, resilient and gifted you really are.

## My Tools & Rituals to Stay in the Flow

There's nothing that serves me more than this one thing. It's two questions. The first one is: "Where am I?" That has to do with being conscious of where my awareness is. One of the things that I learned a long time ago is that when I get overwhelmed, it means I'm not present. I'm just not here. So much of the time we're not in our bodies at all.

When I ask myself the question "Where am I?" it's to bring my awareness, which depending on the stress level, may be over across the room or it may be down the street. Your awareness isn't attached to your body at all. You could send it to Hawaii right now. You just thought of the beach and palm trees, right? See!

In order to be fully present, you have to be in the body first. Ask yourself the question, "Where am I?" and just pause and feel for wherever your awareness is without trying to change it. Then once you have a hold of it, and if you're doing this for the first time, it may take you a couple of tries, but wherever it is, then see if you can invite it into your body.

For me the place that really makes the difference is the solar plexus, which is in the upper abdomen. That's above your belly button and below your diaphragm. That is where the soul resides. It's imperative for you to take up all that space because if you're not, other people are.

The second question is: "When am I?" It is an awkward question. It has to do with am I in this moment; am I in the past; or am I in the future? My experience is you can't be in the present moment unless you're in the body.

When you're overwhelmed, you're in the future. Not only are you in the future, but you're in a future in which you've already failed because you're envisioning that you blew it. Saying things to yourself like "I didn't make that deadline" or "I screwed up." All of that is what creates the overwhelm.

When you stop, breathe and get in your body; in that moment, you know what to do next. Then you know what's that next perfect step for you to take. And all you ever need to do is the next step. That is my favorite process that I still use to this day, and sometimes multiple times a day.

## My Purpose Is

My system is called Divine Navigation. We have just celebrated the eighth anniversary of when it was dropped in my lap from the heavens and started teaching me how it works.

We have two primary ways that we work with people doing the same exact thing, but they have two different outcomes that they want. We have a personal path and a business path.

On the personal side of things, we work with people who are quite successful and their life really pretty much works. They think "what do I have to complain about?" "Why can't I just be satisfied?" "I have all the stuff that I'm supposed to want, right?" Yet they still have that quiet little voice inside that tells them there's something missing.

On the business path, we work with transformational entrepreneurs to make sure they're running the business that their soul wants them to, not just the one they think they have to, to make money. The foundational work is exactly the same for both paths.

What we do is identify the specific energetic qualities of your soul, your Divine Coordinates®, so that you know exactly what will fulfill you because no matter what you try there's absolutely nothing else that will. No amount of achievement, accomplishment or acquisition is going to fill this hole in your soul where you belong.

Women are taught to tend and nurture and there's all these expectations. There are the expectations from society, from our family, and the ones we put on ourselves to be super woman in a way that doesn't serve us.

When we know who we are at an energetic soul level, we can stop trying to be anything other than that. That is what is required to have fulfillment in your life and success in your business. You can get that externally referenced success but that does not bring satisfaction.

## My Gift for You

There are two pathways to choose from: the personal path for personal wellbeing and fulfillment, or the business path. If you're running a business where you feel like you're working way too hard for the results you're getting or you're not getting results even though you're doing everything right, the business pathway is a great one for you to choose.

Once you select the pathway, we're going to walk you through more about how the Divine Coordinates work and you'll also get a really powerful centering exercise. The centering exercise will help you connect and begin to wake up and activate your Divine Coordinates within you.

There are quite a few other things on each pathway, but I'll let you see what those are when you access them.

Grab your gift from Ronda Renee at: www.SuperwomanBook.com/gifts

## My Advice for You in Your Journey

For me, I think the thing that always comes up is to remain centered on yourself. We have this taboo of being self-centered. My question always is, "Well, who else would you like to be centered on?!"

Personally, I'm going to pick me.

It may feel like a luxury, but it's a necessity to give yourself that space to be able to connect with yourself and get authentic about what you want from an internal space instead of that external reference. Then move in alignment with that.

Take the time to be quiet every day and do that connecting with yourself so that you can move through your life in a way that really serves you and not just everybody else.

It may feel like a luxury, but it's a necessity to give yourself space to be able to connect with yourself and get authentic about what you want from an internal space instead of that external reference.

~ Ronda Renee

# THE 30% CRITICAL MASS MOVEMENT

## I am a stand for powerful women being seen.

*Mari-Carmen Pizarro*

## My Superwoman Breakthrough

My breakthrough moment happened three years ago.

I had been in the corporate leadership arena for twenty-eight years, working with executive men and women. But somehow lately I ended up attracting more and more women.

For a year and a half, I worked with a group of eighteen women. These powerful executives were highly educated, confident, and well-respected in their organizations. They were all close to getting their next promotion. (Or, in some cases, their last promotion was the CEO position.) They were rock stars in their fields.

As their careers grew, every one of them was told—mostly by other well-intentioned women—that they needed to be stronger, more confident, bolder, louder, and harder-working than men just to be noticed. The truth is that these women did work harder than any man in their organizations. I did the same thing when I worked in a corporate environment. However, these ladies were bitter, unhappy, exhausted, and frustrated.

They had another thing in common. All these women had been hired by, and reported to, a male manager. The two CEOs reported to an all-male board of directors. In corporate, that is actually the norm.

But here's the beautiful thing. Their male bosses are the ones who brought me in to work with these women. These men cared for and respected the women they worked with.

When I asked the men about their goals for these women, they gave the best responses. One man said, "She can potentially replace me." Another said, "She can have the international assignment that she's been looking for, and I can't wait to give it to her." While not everyone had specific goals, the overall desire was for these ladies to rock it and to be happy and less guarded.

These guys were the women's biggest fans. They also knew that these women were stuck. The men all said that the issue wasn't performance related. Rather, they had an impression that something was "off"—that some of the women took things too personally and others seemed too distracted.

I became an advocate for these ladies. In our one-on-one coaching, things eventually got raw and difficult. I knew that it was time for them to look in their own mirror and see if they might be doing something that sabotaged their goals. When that happened, each one of these eighteen powerful women pushed back and closed off. So I lovingly challenged them back.

They all shared a similar response—that maybe they hadn't gotten what they wanted because they were women. I heard that statement repeatedly over the eighteen months that we worked together. "Maybe it's because I am a woman."

My heart broke into small pieces. I realized is that these ladies' perceived glass ceiling was so real for them that it affected the way they acted. It affected the way other people perceived them in the organization. They were not shining the way they were supposed to shine!

So that was the first big break. We could work with their limiting beliefs, but there had to be something more to it.

I went on a mission to figure this out. I'm all about data. My company joined forces with Mckinsey Global Institute, a global leadership company that had the resources that we didn't have alone to do research.

In a three-year global research study, they discovered that there are nine essential global leadership behaviors. They are: developing people, creating expectations, creating reward systems, role modeling, participatory decision making, effective communication, intellectual stimulation, taking corrective action when necessary, and individual decision making.

Out of these nine behaviors, women naturally apply five of them more often than men:

- people development
- creating clear expectations
- creating reward systems
- role modeling
- participatory decision making.

Out of the remaining four behaviors, men and women apply two of them equally.

When I learned about this study, I was certain now that it was not about being stronger or louder or bulldozing our way to the top.

Armed with this data, I created a process of professional and personal development geared to highlight those behaviors that women do more naturally than men, and to develop the other four.

These revelations took me more into more sociopolitical work and my business shifted again a little. I started getting involved with work at the United Nations, and I discovered that closing the gender gap globally can bring $12 trillion to the global economy. The goal is to do that by the year 2025.

Imagine the type of infrastructure that we can create with this money: day care in the office, flexible work schedules, home offices, drivers for the children's activities. It's a working mother's dream.

It's not about a 50/50 split when it comes to the gender gap. We just need to have 30% of women in senior leadership positions to shift productivity, profitability, and innovation. That is called the 30% Critical Mass.

In the top Fortune 500 companies in the US today, 6% of CEO's are women; 94% are men. But we only need 30% to reach that critical mass; we don't even have to shoot for 50/50.

This theory is that, almost across the board, when there's less than 20% participation from women, nothing much changes. Women don't speak up, or we speak up and we're not heard. Now, anywhere between 25%-30% is where the magic happens. That critical mass is obtained, and suddenly our voices are heard.

So whether it's on a military campus, in the Senate, on a corporate board, or in small businesses, groups function better with diversity. The diversity I'm talking about today is female diversity.

So based on this data, I completely modified what I did with these eighteen executive women. I developed the program that I still teach today. They developed the skills that came naturally to them. They stopped trying to act like men, and they joined forces with other ladies in the organization to create that critical mass. (One thing that I discovered, sadly, is that sometimes women are other women's worst enemies.)

Now these female executives are re-energized and happy. They shattered their glass ceilings, and they're killing it in their organizations.

## My Tools & Rituals to Stay in the Flow

I do a lot of work with stress management, especially meditation. It helps me to be on my best game and to be confident. Other people may prefer a few minutes of time alone, journaling.

I also help women to tap into their femininity. One of my (male) mentors once said, "Until you start believing that you're a powerful woman and not a guy, and until you start using your femininity, you're going to struggle and be frazzled." It's just what these women did.

It's no wonder women get to a point where there are no more promotions. They're too scared and frazzled. Tapping into their femininity is a game changer.

## My Purpose Is

I work mainly with organizations, intact teams and do one-on-one coaching. I also work with business owners who are starting to grow their teams. That's when their weaknesses and lack of formal leadership training becomes evident.

I close the gap using a step-by-step process of specific strategies that are based on research and data. We assess where you are, then we remove all the obstacles that get in the way. We rebuild the new leader that is ready to take on a team and to build the business to whatever level they want to take it.

## My Gift for You

This resource came out of my own struggles with persuasion. I'm a very confident person. I can be assertive, bordering on aggressive. But I wasn't always persuasive. I started to systematically learn how to become persuasive so that others would listen to what I had to say.

I created The Ultimate Persuasion Blueprint. It tells you exactly what to do before you go into any persuasion conversation—whether it's with your children, with your husband, with your team, or with CEOs of fortune 500 companies.

It tells you how to prepare ahead of time, what to do during the conversation, and what to do after. It helps you create a standard operating procedure for these conversations. Every time I follow it, I nail it.

Grab your gift from Mari-Carmen Pizarro at: www.SuperwomanBook.com/gifts

## My Advice for You in Your Journey

Know what you are good at and own it. Don't try to be something you're not. Go with the current of your brilliance and enjoy the process. Changing the world becomes possible when we work from this place instead of against it.

Know what you are good at and own it. Don't try to be something you're not.

~ Mari-Carmen Pizarro

# STARTING OVER FROM OVERWHELMED POLICE OFFICER TO EMPOWERED ENTREPRENEUR

I am my biggest asset and honor myself.

*Diane Halfman*

## My Superwoman Breakthrough

I feel like every woman has this turning point in their life. For me it was when I was still with the police department as an undercover police officer. I worked gangs, narcotics, vice, and I also worked on patrol.

In that time, I got into a training accident and shattered my gun hand. I lost the use of my right hand and being right-handed I had to relearn how to use everything with my left hand. From getting dressed, to writing, to managing toilet paper, all the daily things that we can take for granted in our life.

I had some time to reflect and realized in the ten years I had been on the department; I was a single mom with two young daughters and just trying to make my life work. I was working all the time.

I realized at the time of my accident that I was just exhausted and overwhelmed. During recovery, I noticed how drained I actually was and took stock of my life. What I learned from that was that I am the asset. If I am broken down and not working, then I am no good to anybody else.

I started treating myself as that asset in my work as an officer, in my business, as an entrepreneur, even in my training. It's knowing that I need to fill myself up first. It's in that overflow that I'm able to support everybody else that I'm here to serve.

## My Tools & Rituals to Stay in the Flow

What I have found is that when I feel the most overwhelmed, is when I haven't given myself enough space, such as overloading my calendar. If that happens and I've got too much happening, I feel like I literally can't breathe. When I notice that I'm feeling overwhelmed or even if I'm procrastinating on things or things aren't working, then I realize that there's too much happening, and I've not given myself some space.

The tool that I've created around that to help give me that space is I use the acronym of PIES. It is a check-in with myself where I look at each area that includes the letters in PIES.

The P for my physical body. I just do a scan and go, okay, what's happening? Am I getting enough rest and am I feeding myself? Do I have any aches and pains? I just notice what's happening with that.

Then the I is for my intellect. What's happening in my mind? Am I having thoughts racing through my mind? Do I

145

need to do a brain dump to get everything out? Am I not able to think because I've got so many things happening in my mind and I bring awareness to that?

And then the E is for emotional, like what is happening in my emotions? Am I not expressing emotion? Am I feeling emotional? What is happening to allow myself to have that experience? When you actually express an emotion and it moves through you, you can be more present.

When you go through all three of those, just asking a scan for yourself in that area, then you're able to get to the S, which is the spiritual message that you have. It's that inner knowingness that we have. Typically, we don't need to have more knowledge, it's just accessing our inner knowing, our wisdom and giving ourselves the space to just ask. What is the next step? What is the next message for me? By creating and utilizing that process, you're able to get that message so that you're clear on what is the next step for you.

## My Purpose Is

I'm a keynote speaker and workshop leader and I support corporate and entrepreneurial women so that they can be stronger, safer and be seen in the world.

Particularly in this #MeToo environment, I have women look at what's next. I now support a movement called "Not Me" and the Not Me is where we're setting the boundaries to be strong women, to really start seeing how we're claiming our space.

I teach some tools about how to be a commanding leader in your realm of who you are with fierceness but doing it with femininity. The goal is to still be approachable and not intimidating.

I think it's so important for women to stand in their power. One of the things I teach are three key self-defense moves because I think if women know how to take care of themselves, it builds their confidence.

You actually show up differently in the room and you feel like you can protect yourself in your environment with anyone. I teach how to position yourself to not get into compromising positions in the first place.

I think giving women the tools to really stand in who they are with structures and being more organized, so they feel more empowered and confident claiming their space, allows them to step into their leadership more powerfully.

## My Gift for You

My gift is about the five moves to reset your power. One of the things around power is that we all have that power within us. We came here with it and it's only the layers of things that happen in our life where it gets taken away from us. It can often feel like we're giving our power away and I show people how to stand in their power.

In my gift, I include a simple five step checklist where you can reset that power and start noticing where you're giving your power away, how to access that inner knowing and to really simplify things.

When we make things complicated, it makes it so much more challenging for ourselves. It's important to see what our power habits are, how to get in the zone and stay there, and create the environment that supports us in our life.

Grab your gift from Diane Halfman at: www.SuperwomanBook.com/gifts

## My Advice for You in Your Journey

I think the most important thing is to be in community. I think whether or not you are an entrepreneur or you're in a corporate position, sometimes it can feel isolating. Either you're the only woman in the room or you're the only woman behind the computer and it is really important to create a community of support.

It's powerful to have cheerleaders that really move you forward because the entrepreneurial and corporate journey is very much a rollercoaster ride. To have people that support you along that way in that journey, whether they're by having mentors or accountability partners or just dear friends is ideal. You don't want to do it alone, it's powerful to have people that get you and have your back.

One of my favorite quotes that I like to share is from Clement Watt, which is "Take the first step. No more, no less, and the next will be revealed." It's taking that first step. And when you do that, it allows you to then see the next step in the picture. You don't need to know all the different steps. Just take the first step and the next step will be revealed.

You don't want to do it alone, it's powerful to have people that get you and have your back.

~ Diane Halfman

# SELF-FORGIVENESS
# OPENS THE DOOR
I am open to receiving.

*Michelle Atlas*

## My Superwoman Breakthrough

For years, I tried every tip, tool and recommendation to grow my business. I swallowed whole all the advice in the marketplace. Nothing daunted me. I mastered one enormous learning curve after another. I made money, but the return on my investment never felt like it matched the immense effort I put in.

I didn't realize that with each mountain I climbed I was slipping further away from my own soul and the essence of who I really am.

I lost touch with my natural success pattern, my authentic self-expression and my real gifts.

Until I awoke one day, to a roaring voice within, screaming, "This is not working!"

That clarity catalyzed some major changes. I sold my house, downsized radically and changed the alchemy of my life and business. I rested into my one-on-one work with clients, which I had always loved, and coasted for a while, allowing my whole being to reconfigure.

When I was ready to reemerge, I made a significant financial commitment to a wonderful coach. Since I had received a major financial commitment simultaneously, from a new client, I was confident this would work out perfectly.

But when my new client fell through, there was a point at which I was unable to fulfill my financial commitment to my coach.

As someone who prides herself on keeping promises and following through with agreements, this circumstance was everything I had always dreaded!

It triggered every moment of shame, abandonment, and disloyalty that I'd experienced as a child. Feelings of unworthiness, insecurity, and self-loathing rushed in and overwhelmed me like a tsunami.

I've been dedicated to personal transformation since I was about thirteen years old. But here was another layer of the onion, bringing another opportunity to recycle some very toxic messaging.

My profound healing money breakthrough began when my coach met me with deep understanding and love and held space for my growth.

I rapidly moved from intense negativity and fear to a place of abiding peace and well-being—and a very deep level of fearlessness. My fear just evaporated.

My self-trust returned in a way that I had never quite experienced. I've always had a high-risk tolerance, able to endure a lot of ups and downs. But I was now in a place of complete peace.

I had a vision of myself falling backwards with my arms wide open and landing on a white feather pillow. I felt this incredible softness, safety, openness, and fearlessness.

Within a very short time, a week or ten days at the most, money started pouring in effortlessly from all directions. People I'd never met showed up and hired me for my high-end, one-on-one work. I suddenly received a significant royalty check for work I had done an entire year earlier. I officiate sacred ceremonies and it seemed every day somebody texted me wanting me to marry them. I had one of the best months in the history of my business. And the month after that was even better.

I was able to fulfill my commitment to my coach, while experiencing a level of internal transformation that's really hard to put into words.

I released a lifetime of shame through self-forgiveness and self-acceptance. That's a key part of the work that I do with my clients. It's the missing link for a lot of people.

You can focus on manifesting. You can become an expert on all kinds of services. But if there are self-forgiveness blocks, you can't receive the unlimited good that is always available to you—the door is locked. Self-forgiveness opens your heart to yourself, which is how you become available to money, love and well-being.

## My Tools & Rituals to Stay in the Flow

I feed my spirit by spending time on things that take me out of my mind-space and into my heart-space, my creative flow-space. I'm an artist at heart, but I was so focused on my business for years that I neglected those parts of myself—the musician, the artist, and other parts of who I am.

I began to bring those elements back into my life, weaving them in weekly. Sometimes that means working less so that I can do other things. I have found that my money flow has absolutely nothing to do with how hard I work. So I've begun to work less, in order to embrace more richness and meaning in my day-to-day life.

The experience of abundance in the form of creative fulfillment, attracts abundance in other forms, such as money. It raises my frequency, and like harmonizes with like. If I'm denying and abandoning those parts of myself, then it shows up in the form of scarcity in other ways too.

I've also been meditating religiously since I was nineteen and greatly value time in nature.

These days, I focus more on receiving and allowing than on getting. Sometimes our efforts to manifest lead to pushing and reaching for things. We may even try to manifest a fantasy that we don't have a connection to. Focusing on the fullness in this moment can increase both richness and riches.

## My Purpose Is

I help creative, intuitive women entrepreneurs free themselves from everything that's not them, so that they can create change that they did not think possible in their relationship to money, love, and themselves.

I help my clients transform their feelings of unworthiness and doubt into self-love, authenticity and an empowered relationship to money, so that their business goals, their personal growth goals and their souls calling become one and the same. This is how we become magnetic to all forms of good, of abundance.

I also work with people who are navigating significant transitions—personal or professional changes or losses to help them grow through life's difficulties.

## My Gift for You

One of my other business breakthroughs occurred several years ago, through taking a money archetype quiz. I am a licensed in this money archetype system (authored by Kendall

Summerhawk). This quiz turns the lights on and will help you understand your money personality. I'd love you to take the money quiz for free.

When you take the quiz, you'll receive automated results with a snapshot of your money personality. You'll learn a lot about yourself.

Grab your gift from Michelle Atlas at: www.SuperwomanBook.com/gifts

## My Advice for You in Your Journey

Begin listening more deeply within to where you feel most alive and in your own flow. Trust yourself, your intuition, your inner guidance. Pull back from the hype outside of yourself. You are the best expert on yourself. Only when you come home to who you really are, can you create a business that makes money easily and naturally. Your business can be a path that brings you home to your own heart and body. It can be inseparable from what you want and love most in life.

Begin listening more deeply within to where you feel most alive and in your own flow. Trust yourself, your intuition, your inner guidance. Pull back from the hype outside of yourself.

~ Michelle Atlas

# BREAK THROUGH TO BREAK FREE
## I am living my soul's purpose.

*Sabine Messner*

## My Superwoman Breakthrough

As an embodied soul who is in business with her purpose, I never identify with temporary feelings of success or failure. There is no success or failure in my life, only breakthroughs. I break through to break free. For me, breakthroughs are synonymous with creating prosperity and unlimited inner and outer freedom.

When I was a teenager, I pledged that I would always live in such a way that I could die any day knowing that I have lived my greatest and brightest purpose. I lived according to that pledge and, as a consequence, had a beautiful, brave and brazen life. Because when you put your soul's purpose before logic and reason, the mundane, the stereotypes, and all the other mental excuses, you very quickly become a divinely-guided person.

When I started with my business, my first big breakthrough was aligning my business model and services as closely with my soul's purpose as I could. My next biggest breakthrough was creating a highly sustainable, part-time six+ figure income by continuing to expand on that purpose. I had always been in touch with my soul's calling but I wasn't exactly creating wealth. So my quest became to break free internally and financially—both. I call it "liberating my prosperity."

I discovered two secrets to fulfilling that quest. First, I branded my business as Soul Purpose Branding®, which is the art of claiming your genius expertise and coining it in a brand that's memorable and timeless. In this way, I've helped hundreds of entrepreneurs and coaches in the expert industry position and differentiate themselves.

The second key was the creation of Soul Purpose Wealth™ which is the inner and outer ability to generate and receive all the money and abundance that you ever need or desire. So first, you need to understand who you are, and what you're all about. As it is said, "Know thyself." That knowledge forms the core of your brand, which then generates Soul Purpose Wealth.

That is, for me, the definition of not only financial freedom but true prosperity—that I don't have to do a bunch of things to be successful. I can create it in such a way that I am joyous and playful, while I continue to live prosperously.

## My Tools & Rituals to Stay in the Flow

We have received so many tools—the five steps to this, and the secret formulas for that, and on and on. They are the basis of the "niching game" we've been playing and the inspiration for my contrarian branding and positioning philosophy.

For years, like so many of my colleagues and peers, I too overdosed on these so-called secrets and insider tips. Then I stripped it all back to a blank slate—which was all I needed to be creative, efficient, and effective with my manifestations. I now believe that there is no one-size-fits-all solution.

However, the one tool I go by is Human Design which I've studied for years with a master teacher. I am now able to give incredible Human Design Soul Activations. They're not just readings; they truly activate your soul. When I reveal a person's unique Human Design, we discover what makes you tick. Then you just do more of that. And before you know it, you don't need checklists, secret formulas, and all of those mechanics. You are naturally returning to your divine flow.

Each person is intrinsically different. Over time, the productivity tools that work for a Generator can make a Projector die of cancer or create other serious physical issues for them. Knowing your Human Design is vital—not only for your success but literally for your physical, emotional and spiritual survival.

We need to look at the longevity of our bodies and our overall well-being, not just our businesses. We can't always put the business first and then suffer the consequences. We've had to say goodbye to too many colleagues because they did just that. It's sobering.

Please, investigate very carefully before you admit to "rules and guidelines" that you're living by. If in doubt, eliminate them. Go back to your source. Plug into your soul. You can't go wrong when you follow your soul's protocol.

## My Purpose Is

I work with new business owners to help them find their soul's purpose and tap into their entrepreneurial potential at the beginning of their journey. I also work with more seasoned and experienced entrepreneurs to refine or reinvent their brand and message for greater impact, and more financial freedom and inner fulfillment.

We always start by diving into a person's soul, that reservoir where their deepest dreams, desires, and treasures are hidden. My brilliance is to trace these gifts and liberate them, and then to directly translate them into the correct brand and business model for your soul. We also take into consideration your Human Design and based on that innovate intuitive marketing methods that are in alignment with your innate nature. The key is to never get trapped by cookie-cutter strategies and generic approaches.

People work with me for a minimum of six months. They come out knowing 100% who they are and what they are supposed to do in the world. Usually, the business and the brand we define are timeless which gives my clients that deep knowing and grounding that lets them overcome challenges with conviction and courage. I always look for the things that are evergreen. Everything evolves and becomes more refined over time. But I go right to that core essence that, once you know it and work with it, sustains you for the rest of your life.

## My Gift for You

My gift is called Prosperity Liberation. It's a brand-new webinar that is super timely and powerful. It takes a close look at the archetypes of Feminine Money Shadows that hold us women back from stepping into greater wealth. On the journey to a sustainable multiple-six-figure income, you need to face certain shadows. I talk about exactly what they are so that you can address them and liberate yourself quickly and efficiently.

Grab your gift from Sabine Messner at: www.SuperwomanBook.com/gifts

## My Advice for You in Your Journey

Live your soul's purpose. Nothing gives you more freedom and fulfillment.

Live your soul's purpose.
Nothing gives you more
freedom and fulfillment.

~ Sabine Messner

# SAYING YES TO MY DREAMS
## I am capable of doing anything I set my mind to.

*Keri McGinn*

## My Superwoman Breakthrough

My childhood was constant chaos. I grew up in a very dysfunctional environment, to say the least.

My mother had bipolar disorder and battled addiction. My father struggled with PTSD. So things weren't always great at home. My older sister left home at fourteen, and my younger brother left soon after. My mother left us when I was sixteen years old.

As a young girl and into early adulthood, I constantly tried to get ahead, find ways to break the cycle, be the good kid, and make the right decisions in the midst of family chaos.

I couldn't attend college even though I was a great student. I had to work full time. At nineteen, I found my boyfriend, the love of my life. I put myself on hold for him a lot.

When college became feasible, I shelved the idea because he was going to medical school. I felt that his education was more important to our relationship than mine. That decision took me on a career path that I did not enjoy.

I started out as a secretary and ended up as an acting general manager for a junk removal company with one of the largest territories in the franchise. Even without a college degree, I attained this position of leadership. I made a good living.

Then I hit my first wall.

I had a company car, which meant I had to go wherever I was told to go. I had the company phone, which meant I had to answer that phone whenever it rang. I found myself completely wiped out.

To make matters worse, I had no management skills or experience at the time. As the operations manager, my boss expected me to oversee a team of fifteen twenty-year-old men who did a physical labor job that I'd never done. I needed to do logistics for this team even though I had no idea how to do the job. I didn't have the experience to lead these guys.

It was a very difficult and chaotic time for me—trying to run a business in a bad economy and trying to be a new wife to a husband who was not very present.

Throughout my life, my stress has always manifested in a very physical manner. I am the kind of person who will break out in hives, even though I think everything's fine. Or my palms will constantly sweat. I think that, because I've always absorbed the stress of my environment, I internally manifest it.

So I scratched and clawed my way through that time, but it took its toll on me physically. I could not sleep. I tried Ambien®, but it didn't help. And at that time in my life, I was not the kind of person who could meditate.

I thought, "I can't do this anymore." It's unhealthy to not sleep. The human brain cannot function appropriately. I couldn't have a relationship or perform at my peak performance when I wasn't getting the rest I needed.

As a last-ditch effort, I tried flotation therapy.

During my first session in a float tank, I experienced such peace and clarity of mind. I had my best night's rest in a long time. I realized the harm I was doing to myself, putting myself through the ringer for a career for which I had no passion.

I've always had a passion for helping people, which is why I was always drawn to positions that allowed me to be a right-hand man. I felt like my work as an operations manager was not in alignment with what my heart yearned to do.

As I continued flotation therapy, I realized that this is in alignment with who I am. I understood that I didn't need to push myself so hard for someone else when I could work for myself instead. I've always given 110% effort to everything I've done. I could do this for myself.

Philadelphia had no place to float at the time. I first had my first float experience in a float tank showroom where a gentleman built the tanks. It wasn't the most relaxing experience, but desperate times called for desperate measures.

I realized that other people need access to this resource, too. So I opened a float center and created a space of healing for other people. I could be of service to them in that way.

During my first year of business, I had another big epiphany. My doors opened in March of 2014. By May of 2014, my husband at the time said, "I don't want to do this field of medicine anymore. I want to go back to school and be a different type of doctor."

At that point in my life, I had put everything on hold for him. The year before, I had been brave enough to say, "I want to do this for myself. You went to medical school, you had your residency, and we have a house now. You have your job; you're good to go for two years. I'd like to pursue my dream now."

When he asked me to put my dream on hold for him again, only two months after I opened my shop, it was a wake-up call.

I said, "Hell no! I can't be in this situation anymore. I am not just here for that purpose. I have my own drive, my own heart, my own spirit path to follow. I cannot keep putting myself on the back burner like this."

He didn't understand at all. It dawned on me that our relationship had been very one-sided for a long time. So I did the hardest thing I've ever done in my life. I left my marriage.

I felt excruciating heartache with that decision. I lost everything. I couch-surfed with friends for a year. But it cracked open a new world for me. I broke into a million pieces, and that those pieces turned into the soil that grew the seed that I am now.

I feel like I'm a blossoming flower. All the struggles that I went through in opening my shop and ending my marriage showed me what I could do for myself.

Since then, I feel like there's nothing I can't do. I learned so much about myself from those "failures." I see them as opportunities now. All the struggles have been a blessing.

## My Tools & Rituals to Stay in the Flow

I'm blessed that my path and my business align with my personal healing. I use my float tanks as often as possible, usually once a week. I take ninety minutes out of my schedule each time. It's very much a ritual for me. I leave my cell phone behind and I don't think about work or anything else. I go in the tank and unplug.

Sometimes I fall asleep. Sometimes I force myself to be very present, full of gratitude, and appreciate every second of that ninety minutes. Sometimes I let my mind wander to explore what pops up. That time is invaluable to me. It keeps me centered, grounded, and grateful.

It also helps me release the physical manifestations I experience from holding in stress. It takes me out of my environment and forces me to let those things go. So I'm physically healthier as a result. Floating in the float tank is an excellent tool for that.

You can have a similar experience through meditation, running, or o yoga. I cannot emphasize enough how getting out of your environment and into your own personal zone is crucial to being a productive, happy human.

## My Purpose Is

I'm the owner of Halcony Floats where I help people experience Floating or Sensory Deprivation Therapy. It is a relaxation and healing practice that involves restricting sensory input to achieve a deepened meditative state and pain relief. Our custom float rooms are filled with ten inches of a highly concentrated Epsom saltwater solution. The density that results from almost 1,300 pounds of Epsom salt makes you completely buoyant as the healing solution supports your entire body along it's natural supine curvature; you're weightless in the float.

The solution is skin sensor neutral, about 93.5 to 95.5 degrees, so you lose physical sensation of your own body, including aches and pains you may be used to feeling. The float spaces are sound-proof and quiet, lights can be turned off to achieve the perfect environment to rest the senses. Within the first thirty minutes of your float, you notice a dramatic drop in your stress level and an increase in your overall serenity, as the Epsom Salt solution works to heal and detox your body, and the floating position releases tension and pressure from your joints and muscles.

I encourage you to find a local center to experience the benefits of Floating for yourself.

## My Gift for You

People often ask me why they should float. So I created a reference guide that tells you the top twelve ways that floating can change your life.

Grab your gift from Keri McGinn at: www.SuperwomanBook.com/gifts

## My Advice for You in Your Journey

Listen to yourself. I know it sounds cliché, but you have a responsibility to yourself. You cannot be there for anyone else until you are full within your own heart and mind. Do not deny yourself the personal care of listening to yourself.

Also, failures are just building blocks. They are steppingstones along the way. Every time you hit a wall, know that it's there to prove how much you want something, and what you are capable of. So be in tune with yourself. Don't be hard on yourself. Take care of yourself and learn from your mistakes.

You cannot be there for anyone else until you are full within your own heart and mind. Do not deny yourself the personal care of listening to yourself.

~ Keri McGinn

# REDEFINING YOUR FORMULA FOR SUCCESS
### I am me, amplified.

*Angela Chee*

## My Superwoman Breakthrough

My biggest breakthrough happened about six years ago. My kids were three and five years old, and I felt really burned out. I remember sitting on the couch, just feeling blah. I had left my full-time job as a TV news anchor a few years before and started a blog. I was also coaching and speaking on the side. I was writing all the time for different sites, doing videos, keeping up with social media, trying to be there for my kids, and trying to do it all.

I would take care of my kids in the day. At night, I worked on my articles and other projects just to keep my voice alive. I stayed up late every night and I was exhausted.

While I enjoyed the freedom of my new journey, leaving daily live TV, I felt like I lost a bit of my voice. Blogging and building the online part of my business was a way to connect with people and continue to share.

But in reality, I hadn't built a business yet. I was blogging and chasing a whole bunch of to do's. I was living by my old formula of success. The more things I could check-off. The more I could get done. Meant more achievement and equaled more success.

I grew up with Chinese immigrant parents. I worked hard. I'm super independent. As a type-A person, I was used to getting things done all by myself and fast. But as a mom and an entrepreneur, those strategies weren't enough. This old formula of success no longer worked.

I hit a plateau. I had left my job to create a business so I could have flexibility with my family. But in the end, I was exhausted and burned out. I had to create a new formula of success. I needed to redefine what worked for me. Why was I chasing ego? Why was I so driven by those things? What did I really want to say?

That's how my core program, YOU, Amplified!™ came to be. It helps people break through their barriers, turn obstacles into strengths, and get clear on who they are and what really matters. That is success.

What matters to you? What matters to you right now?

That lesson was important for me to learn, and I put it into all of my work.

Who are you? What do you stand for? How do you show up for others? How do you want to feel?

I live my life and build my business around this. Because when you're congruent and clear, you can create an even bigger vision.

Now I live based on my definition of success rather than a checklist.

And by seeing what is possible for yourself, you are empowering others to see what is possible for them.

## My Tools & Rituals to Stay in the Flow

I understand that I'm going to feel burned out occasionally; I'm going to feel down. It's important to recognize when I feel a little bit off, and to honor those feelings. I don't just shoo them away; I actually feel what I need to feel in that moment and notice if those feelings are serving me. Do I need to feel them? Are they guiding me? If not, and if they are stopping me, I need to let that part go.

When I slow down and do that, I can hear more than the external voices around me. I listen to myself. What do I feel? Where is that coming from? Is that coming from me? My past? Society? My cultural background? I've learned to breathe through experiences and process them, instead of powering through them.

I also work on breaking through those barriers both conscious and subconscious. In my early years, my barriers came from my upbringing. I was raised by Chinese immigrant parents and was taught not to rock the boat and play it small.

This year, I'm going even deeper by looking at unconscious barriers in ancestry, in culture, and in the environment—and letting go of those voices and beliefs which are not mine.

I also tap into my joy a lot more and I don't feel guilty about it. I dance, I meditate, I take breaks. I savor moments. I remind myself that it's okay to be joyful. It took a long time to get to that point. So many times, when I get frazzled, I'll stop and ask, "What will bring me joy in this moment? What will move me forward? What are the barriers to doing so?"

## My Purpose Is

I'm a media/communication coach and a keynote speaker. I help visionary women leaders own their voice and their power, step into the spotlight and amplify their message and their missions through speaking, video, and media.

My deeper level work is not just about being a good speaker or being on camera. It's about power, presence and representation. YOU, Amplified!™ is where soul meets strategy. It's about knowing who you are, what you stand for, how you want to be seen. It's about helping people step up into the spotlight and put their work out into the world.

I empower them to be in alignment with themselves. I help them be clear, confident, and connected and ready for any opportunity. Whether they're talking in person, shooting a video, or doing a media interview, I want my clients to feel YOU, Amplified!™ on the inside and the outside so they can create real change.

## My Gift for You

My gift for you is a video series about the YOU, Amplified!™ Formula: The Seven Steps to Confidence, Clarity, and Connection. It's the first step in owning your voice and your power and putting your message out there in a bigger way.

Grab your gift from Angela Chee at: www.SuperwomanBook.com/gifts

## My Advice for You in Your Journey

Take a look inside and know that you already have everything you need to shine and succeed. See it for yourself and amplify it. You've probably heard the call often, but you've second guessed what you're good at and what you've accomplished.

A lot of times, if you're starting something new—whether it's a new job, new business, or motherhood—you tend to forget everything that you've done before. But you're not starting from zero. You have so much more experience than you give yourself credit for.

The key is to see exactly who you are inside, and to understand that you are already complete. Then figure out what you stand for and how you want to put it out into the world to bring it alive. Then make it happen.

You already have everything you need inside to succeed and shine, you just need to discover it for yourself and amplify it!

~ Angela Chee

# THE POWER OF THE LISTENING TOUCH
## I am calm. I am healing.

*Barbara Firer*

## My Superwoman Breakthrough

My mother lived with us for a couple of years after she was diagnosed with ALS. We had been very close. After she passed away, I discovered that I had so many aches and pains, I wasn't functioning physically. I couldn't figure out why.

I knew I didn't need a conventional doctor. I knew I needed someone to help me through my emotional upheaval. In my town, there is a special, holistic therapist who practices CranioBalance. My mom went to her for treatment, and even though she didn't believe in any of it, I saw that she was much more relaxed as a result. So I decided to try it.

CranioBalance is a very light touch therapy. You hardly feel a physical touch, but your body responds by releasing stress and tension. You are filled with calm and well-being.

I saw the practitioner for two sessions. My body felt loose and free. All pain vanished. My thinking became clearer. The solutions to existing problems became straightforward. Almost a week later, I continued to feel an unwinding of my body and mind.

It had such a profound effect on me that I really wanted to learn it. I didn't have any plans of teaching it to anyone. I just needed to know how it worked.

Practicing with a small group of students, I realized how easily these simple techniques can bring calm and well-being to anyone. I thought, "Wow, moms can do this on their babies!"

At that time, my kids were blessing me with a lot of new grandchildren. There was definitely a lot of screaming, and a lack of calm. It brought back memories of my own kids as babies, and how they cried for hours and hours.

So I started using the technique on my grandchildren. It actually worked! It brought calm to the baby and the family. I learned that there doesn't have to be a crying hour.

I believe that anyone can do this, not only therapists. So I took this simple technique and passed it on to moms, to empower them with their babies.

## My Tools & Rituals to Stay in the Flow

I do a lot of mind work, a lot of self-support, a lot of "I can do this." It may not be perfect, and I might not be perfect, but whatever I do will help. Each time, I get better at supporting myself.

Although there is definitely a place for traditional medication and advice to treat illness, many ailments are based on stress and fear. You can learn to relax your mind by placing your hands gently on points of pain.

## My Purpose Is

I teach moms about The Listening Touch—how to use their hands to listen to their babies' bodies. It doesn't mean squeezing, pulling, or pushing. It is a very light touch. Sometimes you don't even have to touch at all. You learn to feel sensations that the body produces.

The Listening Touch has many characteristics that make it extremely powerful and healing: using your intuition and feeling safe doing so; using your imagination and visualization, which is a bit like NLP; and self-confidence—knowing that you can do this and that you won't hurt your baby.

When you feel health and well-being, the baby receives it. So I teach the mothers how to release the pain and how to bring well-being into the baby as well. All of those aspects make the healing more powerful. The power of your mind is magical; it can heal your baby.

Moms have a very strong desire to help their babies; it's their maternal instinct. This technique helps the babies connect with their mothers. The babies already trust mom. The moms start off already in a powerful place and they use the Listening Touch to calm their babies. And when the babies calm, the babies heal.

## My Gift for You

I created a course called The Five Steps to Be the Best Mom for Your Baby. It outlines five steps to create calm for your baby. You learn how to be your baby's therapist.

Grab your gift from Barbara Firer at: www.SuperwomanBook.com/gifts

## My Advice for You in Your Journey

Whenever you feel overwhelmed or desperate, there is always a way out. Always. If you feel there is a dead end, know that there is always a way to calm down. When you feel totally overwhelmed, simply stop and start again. Prioritize what you need to do in that moment. Who needs you the most? Sometimes you may need you the most, but each time you prioritize. Trust your intuition, because you will have a gut feeling about what you need to do. Following that gut feeling helps you feel good about the decision.

Figure out step one, then step two. Don't do too many steps, or you'll get overwhelmed again. Just know that there is always a way out. The minute you find it, things become clearer. That's the most important thing, because calm in any shape or form brings both emotional and physical healing. Prioritize healing.

As a family woman, your husband and children will feel your distress. If the kids had been misbehaving because you've been overwhelmed, everything will suddenly seem a little quieter once you become calm again. They reflect how you feel. Our husbands do as well.

Whenever you feel
overwhelmed or desperate,
there is always a way
out.
Always.

~ Barbara Firer

# THROUGH OUR STRIFE
# WE GET OUR STRENGTH
## I am a health activist.

*Louise Swartswalter*

## My Superwoman Breakthrough

I crashed. I was a mom, with two small kids at home. I sought answers for chronic fatigue and MS. I went doctor hopping.

When I say crash, I mean it. I weighed eighty-nine pounds. I lived on oxygen for three years. I was taking care of my two kids at the time and I remember just praying and saying, "All I want to do is be their mom. All I want to do is have my brain working again, have my body working again, and get my health back."

I was also a pesticide activist at the time. They were spraying the lawns in our neighborhood for mosquitoes. Those chemicals made me so sick that I'd have to turn on my oxygen tank. I was so angry about the fact that pesticides are so bad for many people. Many kids have asthma from the products that we use in our environment and pesticides cause cancers.

I became an environmental activist. I worked with our mayor in Schaumburg, Illinois, to sue the state of Illinois. That was the beginning of my speaking. I spoke with my oxygen tank on. I took it with me and I did not care what happened!

I was on a mission to help people understand what was happening in our environment and how it affects our health. So that's how I got into the whole path of natural health.

I worked my butt off. I saw every kind of natural doctor I could possibly find.

My dentist said we should take out all of my mercury fillings. I had bad teeth, so I had fourteen mercury fillings by the time I was twenty-two. What I didn't understand was how toxic those metals could be to my body. My dentist gave me all the literature and convinced me that I should have them all removed in a single day. So I sat in the dentist's chair for six hours.

My whole journey of healing myself took me sixteen years. It taught me the power of following my intuition. It taught me the power of persistence. It made me stronger.

Through our strife, we get our strength.

Eventually I said, "I know all this stuff about natural health now. I think I should have the paper on the wall." So I got a degree in naturopathy. I was introduced to biofeedback, and now I have five different biofeedback devices that help people all over the globe.

So my health crash became the trajectory that turned the tables around in my life. In 1994, we moved my whole family from Illinois to the mountains in Taos, New Mexico, so that I could heal. I call those my Monk Years because we prayed, we saw double rainbows, and we're in this beautiful mountain town. It was completely gorgeous.

After I healed, I yearned to help more people. I started my Albuquerque Natural Health Center business in my home. One of my good friends suggested that I move into an office. I remember being very scared about that. I wondered, "Am I really ready to do that?"

We rented space for seven years, and I did so well that I finally bought my own office. I've seen thousands of clients in the last twenty years, using all the health techniques that I had learned.

In the beginning, I only helped my clients with the body piece—eating, detoxing, and lifestyle changes. These are all important components of healing, but it's not the whole thing.

In my own healing path, I had to change my brain. I had to change my mindset. I had to work on my emotions. I had to work on my spiritual body, and I had to work on the energy field piece. When I started putting all that together with my clients, they changed much more quickly. The results stuck.

That's how my BRAIN System and my Brain-Soul company came to be. BRAIN is an acronym. It stands for Body, Release, Align with spirit, Integrate, and put in a New program. When you do all those steps simultaneously, you get faster results.

I recently had a client who was in the war and had PTSD. He'd felt a pain across his head for ten years. He had done meditation, yoga, therapy, and all the VA therapy that he could do. He spent years doing all those techniques. In a single, two-hour session, the pain went away. It vanished.

The world is really struggling. People want change. They're sick and tired of doctors and pills that don't work. They don't want to take medication. They don't feel good in their own bodies and it's bringing them down. It's time to help people see that there's another alternative, a bigger one than they even thought of. That's the BRAIN system.

## My Tools & Rituals to Stay in the Flow

One of the tools that I use is called Mind Gems. It's twelve little exercises that balance the brain in less than five minutes. I do them in bed before I get up. I do them when I go to sleep. I also do them all day with my clients.

I've even taught them to kids in my school-teaching days. A lot of my students did the Mind Gems before they took a test, and they got better scores.

Another tool that I teach people is how to protect their own energy field. I teach them how to put a "rainbow bubble" around themselves by visualizing themselves in a big rainbow cocoon. The intention is that only love can come in, nothing else. That rainbow cocoon becomes like one of those marbleized, rubberized exercise balls. Especially with kids, negative or harmful vibes bounce off.

My work is called Brain-Soul Balancing. It's a highly intuitive process that helps people release the energy in their field that's blocking them from expressing 100% of their soul's truth. When you can realign and be your soul's truth, you can create anything you want in your life.

For example, if you're thinking about somebody and you can't get them out of your head, you could name a few words about them. They can be positive or negative words. Sometimes you actually feel that person's anger or frustration. Then you might be angry or frustrated yourself, because it's like Velcro®. You caught their feelings.

The process is deeper than that, and it really does clear the brain and soul. But the very first step is to say words about the situation or the person. In other words, speak the truth and you'll feel lighter.


## My Purpose Is

I went from sick to fantastic and now I vibrate at a very high frequency. Clients around the globe come to the USA to experience the BRAIN system. The work has evolved and now I work mostly with business owners and practitioners teaching them the tools of the brain system so they can increase their wealth, finish their books, and up level their life. When they start using the tools with their clients and their patients, they see this big transformation in their whole body and spirit- it is Powerful Positive Healing For Life!

So first, we help them get back to their 100% soul truth. We teach them to hone in on and honor their intuition. They learn how to keep their own energy field clear. They get super healthy—physically, mentally, emotionally, and spiritually. There's always a spiritual component.

I have a year-long program where I teach this process in a certification program. I have several certified Brain-Soul Success coaches who work with these techniques in their own businesses.

## My Gift for You

My gift for you is Mind Gems. It's the piece that is missing in a lot of brain work. So, you can go buy a bottle of supplements to help your memory. You can do Sudoku puzzles and all kinds of little things to help the brain.

The Mind Gems are different because it balances what I call the Brain Rings. It was taught to be my teacher, Dorothy Wood Espiau in the 1980's. Picture an atom. The nucleus of the atom has rings spinning around it. Each one of those rings is, in a sense, spinning around your brain. When they're off-center or wobbly, you won't be balanced.

The Mind Gems help you cross your right and left brain. They help balance the energy field piece of your brain. My clients tell me things like, "I haven't done my Mind Gems on a regular basis. But when I found them today in a stack of papers, I did them and my headache went away." Because they got balanced.

They seem so simple that you might think they're not necessary. So you stop doing them. But when you pick it up again, you see the difference they make.

Grab your gift from Louise Swartswalter at: www.SuperwomanBook.com/gifts

## My Advice for You in Your Journey

Work on staying balanced and always use your tools. I'm not sure even like the word "balance." But the brain is really a control tower for the brain, heart, and gut. There's a little cartoon that I have. It's a picture of a heart and a brain, and it says, "Honor your heart, but take your brain with you."

Work on staying balanced
and always use your
tools.

~ Louise Swartzwalter

# HEALING CANCER & CONNECTING TO MY TRUTH
## I am true to myself.

*Karen Leckie*

## My Superwoman Breakthrough

Years ago, I really burnt out. My mom was sick for three and a half years with a serious lung condition. She was in the hospital and I was the primary caregiver and initially some of that time was in Denmark. She was so sick. She went on a holiday to visit her brothers and sisters in Denmark and then she ended up getting sick there.

I flew over to Denmark and was there for about three months while my mother was in the intensive care unit. Then she came back to Canada. She continued to be sick and it really affected me. I'm a very empathetic person. I'm an empath and

I feel for people. I just went right into that situation with her and I took it on in my own psyche. I took on her struggles, what she was going through and it affected me so much that I had compassion fatigue, but I didn't really think about the consequences to myself when I was in the situation.

I was just in the experience trying to do anything I could to help her. The doctors don't even know how she even got the lung condition. It could have been on the plane while traveling to Denmark. To me, it symbolized grief. She had so much grief in her life with everything that she had gone through.

I also started getting taken over by grief and it was almost like I pre-grieved her loss. I think she just couldn't leave this life. She had a hard time letting go and passing on because she knew how much it would affect me and the entire family. She tried to hold on as long as she could and she lasted three and a half years. During that time, I grieved through the whole thing and she was also grieving and doing a lot of forgiveness work as she was making her transition.

After she passed, my whole world just crashed down. My immune system had been so affected because I had just put my whole life into this. I was a high school teacher at the time, and I had taken a leave and luckily I had very good support. It was just so, so hard for me. After she passed away, I felt incredible guilt for not doing enough. I didn't do enough because I didn't save her! She ended up passing over into heaven and all of the grief took a downturn on my immune system.

Almost six months to the day after she passed, I ended up being diagnosed with breast cancer. I had one loss in my life and then another one came right after it. It seemed like there was no break in between; it was just one thing after another.

What helped me get through it was that I could hear my mom's voice in my head saying, "I want you to take this as a learning experience and from now on, I want you to only choose things that bring you joy in your heart and protect your health. She really, really made a big point about that. Your health is number one. You need to look after yourself." She had said that during the entire time that she was ill and now it really hit home for me.

I think that her passing was a huge turning point for me and triggered a new journey in my life. I needed to do some inner work and emotional healing. I went on a journey to Brazil and Peru to see various healers and started a whole process of discovery and adventure. I wanted to get more in touch with a deeper self-awareness and to cultivate the tools that would really help me, so that later I could teach other people.

## My Tools & Rituals to Stay in the Flow

I have a lot of different tools that I use on a daily basis, and on a monthly basis. In the morning I set a clear intention for my day and I get grounded on my top three goals. I ask myself, what is God's will on my life today??

I start the day by putting out my hand and saying "God, what do you want me to do today?" "God, please guide my steps and order my day." "God, I need you!" A Bible verse that guides me in hearing God's voice to lay down a vision for my life is Habakkuk 2:2 which states "The LORD gave me this answer: Write down clearly on tablets what I reveal to you, so that it can be read at a glance." The tablet is my prayer journal where I record dreams and visions that I hear from God.

Being in the present moment is really important. Whatever you are going through, just face it head on and be in it. I think a lot of times people try to escape it or push it down, and not feel it. That wasn't going to work for me. I knew it wasn't going to work for me. I told myself, "Okay, I'm in this situation, so let's just get grounded in it, and let's go through it." That has helped me. Just being in the present moment has helped me bring a lot of ease and grace and not push so hard all the time.

I do a lot of journal writing and listening to the voice of God. That helps me. On any given day, if I'm having a hard time, I end up crying while I'm writing my journal. If I'm having a good day, then I visualize my goals and see myself doing something that really serves people on a bigger level.

## My Purpose Is

I was my first client in this process. I've taken all of the tools that I helped me in order to help women going through any kind of challenge or major trauma, family situation or illness. I help clients to lay a solid foundation and get clear on their true core so they are able to tap into that on a regular basis. It helps to walk by faith, knowing that God will lead the way and guide your path. I help people receive their miracle so that they can step into God's calling on their life.

I help people clear their past conditioning and do the inner work. Sometimes it involves doing a soul cleanse of things that happened in their family of origin and clearing blocks like self hatred. It also may involve cultivating self-love and setting healthy boundaries. The results that I get with clients is to have people be true to themselves, to get through stressful situations, make conscious decisions, and practice inner contentment. From my Danish heritage, there's a practice called "hygge". The word is kind of like a hug. You might see people post #hygge and it is that feeling of warmth and contentment with life.

Another practice is to create an environment of love in your home. In the winter months you can put up Christmas lights, and little candles around the house to create that feeling of serenity and peace all around. It's something that I've taken from my Danish heritage and brought it into a daily practice to build an environment that supports me.

## My Gift for You

My gift is a dose of courage and a guide for the eight keys to your healing miracle. I believe women are really strong inside and a lot of the time, we already have so much inner strength. However, we shouldn't be too strong for God. Let God support you on your healing journey. Sometimes all it takes is someone to pray for you and give you that little boost.

My gift is to support women with a practice that boosts their courage and reminds them of their inner strength.

Grab your gift from Karen Leckie at: www.SuperwomanBook.com/gifts

## My Advice for You in Your Journey

I've had that rock bottom moment that taught me things that the mountaintop never will. If you are in a moment of your life where you feel hit by the world, try to look for the learning and embrace the gift in the middle of the storm. When I hit rock bottom I was totally lost and I thought that I would never pull out of it. I thought that my world would completely collapse and I didn't even think I could go on. In my darkest moments, I didn't think I would pull through.

Now I teach people how to come out of those moments and realize that after you have been through a trial and been tested, you know your strength in a way that you could never have known without going through it. You have to go through those moments because those moments although they may be tough, are your biggest teachers. It can turn into such a gift and although you can't see it at the time necessarily, later on, upon reflection, you will come to realize that that moment is the greatest gift of your life.

*God doesn't call the qualified but qualifies the called.*

~ Christine Caine

# MY JOURNEY OF FINDING MY TRUE PASSION

## I am creative. I am at peace.

*Lynette Chandler*

## My Superwoman Breakthrough

I am a WordPress designer and developer. I make WordPress plugins. For a time, I had a membership program in which I delivered one new plugin every single month. I've been doing this for ten or twelve years. I love technology and coding. That's me.

A lot of work goes into creating a plugin to begin with. But, there's also a lot of follow-up work. Plugins, like any software, are not something you can just deliver once and then forget about it. Every day, people ask you questions about it. WordPress is huge, with a lot of moving parts. You're not sure if all the pieces will work together. So I need to offer a lot of support.

When my husband developed a serious issue related to his heart where it would go into a seizure of sorts, which could lead to a heart attack, it was a very volatile time. During that time, I started waking up at 2 am or 4 am, several times a week. It was difficult.

Then, we found out my husband wasn't allowed to go back to work, so I needed to ramp up my business. I decided that I was going to enter a business contest. And I thought, "What better way than to challenge myself." I thought the contest would push me to the next level. I thought it was a great idea.

Well, it didn't get off to a great start. There were a lot of things involved in this contest. First of all, I had to submit all kinds of information such as the kind of work I did, and the kind of marketing I did in the last six months. I had to submit a lot of proof. Just submitting the package was a lot of work, in addition to running my business, dealing with my husband's illness, and so on. It was tremendously stressful.

I made it through the first round, and I felt great about it. But then I learned that I needed to give a five-minute presentation on stage, in front of all the judges and the other competitors, to convince them that I deserved the $25,000 cash prize.

I'm a Techie. I've been behind the scenes for a long time. Sure, I could go on a podcast, or even do a video or a webinar with no problem. But being in front of people on stage was totally new to me. That was such a challenge.

Plus, if I went even one second over the allotted time, I'd be automatically disqualified. But there was so much to say. How could I condense everything that I'd done in the last six months into five-minutes? That added extra pressure.

I actually have to thank my husband because not only did he support me, he really pushed me. He pushed me so hard. We have a fantastic marriage. We hardly ever argue, but during that time period, I really wanted to throw something at him. I now look back, and I'm so thankful he pushed me as hard as he did. We rehearsed this five-minute presentation, and we did it as a team, which I am forever grateful for.

On the day of the presentation, I was so nervous. Many people dropped out of the competition that day. In fact, I told my husband that I was going to drop out, too. "I can't do this," I told him. "I just can't."

He said, "Nope, it's too late to turn back now."

So I went up on stage and gave my presentation. And I won! I won the $25,000 cash price. Emotionally, psychologically, it was like a validation of everything I'd worked for all those years.

My children saw me struggle. During that time, they also saw what it takes to succeed. It's not always pretty. It's not always easy. It's not always like the posts on Instagram. It takes a lot of hard work and even more tears.

The win was amazing. But soon after, I actually fell into a depression. I struggled with it for almost a year before I finally decided to go to my doctor.

At first I thought, "Maybe this is just a low. I've been pushing myself so hard. I'm just tired. I need to rest." So, I rested for a month. Then two months went by and things were still lack-luster. I wasn't on fire for my business anymore. I knew that something was wrong in my heart. I still enjoyed coding and technology. But that drive, that fire, that passion and hunger has disappeared.

I thought, "I'll just keep on chugging." I kept delivering products to my customers. Everybody was happy. I had a full-time developer on payroll, and everything on the surface looked good.

But I was shriveling up inside. In a lot of ways, I felt that my work had no purpose. I felt that there was a disconnect in my head. I couldn't get out of the funk, no matter what I did.

I knew that this is not a normal burnout period. I had burnout periods often over the last twelve or thirteen years. They never last this long. It just felt different.

Eventually, I gave in and went to my doctor for help and that set me on the right track.

As a way of coping with my husband's issues and everything else. The pressure, the work, the contest and everything, I really needed to get off my computer. All my work was online. I needed to completely unplug.

I learned how to draw. I doodled in a bullet journal. I penned hand-lettered quotes. I didn't have any idea what I wanted to do with them; I just enjoyed the process. The more I did it, the better I got.

The nice thing about art is that it doesn't have to be perfect. In the tech world, one missing comma can bring down an entire website. I learned to embrace imperfection, and I loved it.

Then I decided, "Maybe this is it. Maybe this should be my other avenue, instead of doing technology. Let's just give it a try and see if I can sell this."

I combined my art and my bullet journal into a planner set—not like regular planners where you have two days to write in, or a calendar. I made something I saw a lot of my friends needed, which is a guided planner. For example, let's say they were starting a podcast. I'd give them a list, suggestions, and then some room for them to write down some of their own ideas.

Even though it's a new venture, it has been such a rewarding experience and I'm very excited about it.

## My Tools & Rituals to Stay in the Flow

Throughout this process, I learned the importance of slowing down. For so long I woke up every morning, hit the ground running, and charged ahead. I realized in that time period that there is a lot of value in just slowing down and taking things one piece at a time, a day at a time, and even an hour at a time.

I had to live hour by hour because I never knew if, in the next hour, I'd get a call and need to go to the emergency room with my husband. It forced me to sit back and say, "Hang on. Maybe you just need to lean back a little bit and pick the things that can propel you further with the smallest amount of time."

I also realized that in this time period, I was still doing little things. A lot of things that we do on a daily basis are not sexy. It's easy to think that those things don't matter. But they do.

It's kind of like a stream that starts from the trickles of water dripping off a tree and then it grows into a tiny little stream. Tiny streams grow into bigger streams and then into rivers. The rivers grow into something like the Amazon. Without those little trickles that come off a tree, you won't have the Amazon. You need all those little streams to get to that huge river.

Instead of waking up, charging ahead, and doing huge things, I began to focus on the little things I could do that would eventually build up.

## My Purpose Is

I create guided planners and journals that you can edit to suit your needs. You can change the name, put your brand on them, and put your own name on them. You can totally re-brand them for yourself. You can use them as lead magnets or give them to your coaching clients as a tool to help them implement what you teach.

Some of my clients build a completely new journal or planner and sell their re-worked product on Amazon and other marketplaces.

Basically, I create the tools that save you time and money on layout, rather than recreating them from scratch. Although, I do have a custom planning program available to coaches and event planners as well.

## My Gift for You

My gift is a webinar planner. In this planner, it will have pages to help you map out your goals and the necessary tasks to get your webinar planned out. There are also review pages, to assess which goals you met, which things worked, what you'd like to change, and whether this something you want to implement again.

Grab your gift from Lynette Chandler at: www.SuperwomanBook.com/gifts

## My Advice for You in Your Journey

Do not despise the small stuff. Sometimes in a daily drudgery of things, it's easy to question whether all the small things you do even matter. They do matter. There is a reward in persistence. Continue with that persistence until it does not pay. Then, in those little small breaks, you may need to take a step back.

Slow down. A lot of times you need to slow down in order to speed up. You don't really know what's happening around you because everything's going by you so fast. But once you slow down, you start noticing things. Maybe you need you stop doing an activity that is no longer working. Or put more focus on a platform that has done very well for you.

But if you constantly keep on producing, you won't have these insights. It's not until you slow down and take careful notice that they pop up.

There is a reward in persistence. Continue with that persistence until it does not pay.

~ Lynette Chandler

# MY JOURNEY FROM MEDICAL DOCTOR TO COACHING FOR INNER PEACE

I am at peace. I am still.

*Dr. Seema Khaneja*

## My Superwoman Breakthrough

The breakthrough that I really felt inspired to share is how I transitioned from being a medical doctor to what I'm doing today, which is coaching.

For medical school and residency, I did my training in top universities such as Mount Sinai Medical School, and New York Hospital-Cornell Medical Center.

But I always inwardly questioned the true nature of healing. How does healing happen? How can I help to facilitate it?

What are the roles of emotions, the mind, the spirit, and spirituality?

So while I was learning Western medicine, I also researched different alternative, complementary therapies. I read books by people like Louise Hay, Deepak

Chopra, and Shaki Gawain.

After I completed my residency in pediatrics, I went on to study holistic medicine and integrative medicine. I added homeopathy, meditation, and Reiki to my practice.

At one point, I got sick and had chronic pain. Nothing I knew helped. I tried to eat the right way. I worked with my homeopath. I had someone help me with the mind-body stuff. I did visualization, yoga—all of it. But healing eluded me. I was in so much pain.

Then I really went deeper, inward. I went into the mind, into beliefs, into ideas about myself. I examined my relationships to everyone in my family, my work, my clients, and my patients. I did a lot of deep, inner digging.

As I did that, my relationship to the pain started to change. The breakthrough moment happened when I clearly understood that it wasn't so much about doing more outer stuff. I had good doctors. I had good people working with me. I didn't need to go to another expert. Instead, I allowed myself the opportunity to be still, as opposed to doing.

I still remember that day. I got up and I just wanted to sit quietly and be in meditation. That moment of stillness was powerful. I felt this sensation of letting go, like a surrender.

For so long, I had told myself, "No, you've got to work hard and you've got to do this and do that. You got to push yourself."

I felt like I'd been swimming upstream for so long, and finally someone said, "Hey, you can just go downstream with the water and let go."

I thought, "Oh my God, I can do that? Is that possible?"

In that moment, I experienced the "peace that passeth all understanding." I felt so much love. All the judgments and ideas—everything just vanished.

In the next couple of weeks, the pain went away. I continued to follow up with my doctors. I still needed to have a minor surgery.

But I knew that something had shifted and that was my breakthrough moment. Now, I needed to do something different.

So, I ended up releasing my western medical job. Ironically, I worked with people who had chronic pain. And I had just become the patient. So this idea of "Physician, heal thyself" took on new meaning. That's actually the name of my upcoming book, which shares this journey.

I was also inspired to create Coaching for Inner Peace, because I felt that the inner journey of healing needs to have attention. How do we nurture that inner journey? What are the roadblocks that people face? What are the places where we could lose our way? What are the supports we need to take that journey?

I felt this desire to share those answers with others who faced their own chronic challenge, whether it was emotional pain or physical pain, or perhaps simply being at a crossroads in their life and seeking a new way to live their lives. With more presence, more awareness, more intention.


## My Tools & Rituals to Stay in the Flow

If we study the whole stress response, we understand the adrenaline surge and those unhealthy stress hormones, versus the relaxation response which we want.

Ultimately, it all starts with your perception of how you see things. Depending on your perception, you have a different experience. Everything I do in my coaching practice is to help you shift your perception.

The journey to love, light, play, peace, and prosperity is often through darkness. It's often through the pain. You don't want to deny the pain; you don't want to put a lid on it. You want to have safe ways to expose it and then allow the healing to come through.

I have lots of heart-to-heart discussions with my clients where they can simply share whatever is coming up for them in their lives. And share all of their emotions and reactions in a safe space where there is no judgment. Just love and acceptance. Journaling is another great way to access emotions and deeper levels of thoughts, beliefs and desires.

I also do a lot of guided meditation to help my clients come to that space of stillness. I also encourage people to exercise—gentle walks, yoga, or other mind-body movement exercises where they can slow down and just be with themselves and give themselves that space of quiet.

And I also love sharing inspiring movies. Watching other people who might be negotiating what you're negotiating in life is a way to step back and shift your perception.

I try to make the tools very organic to what people are drawn to. You know, not everyone likes to journal; not everyone likes to meditate. The whole idea is to discover how you can be with yourself, get to know yourself. What's in your heart, and what are you afraid of? Then, beneath that, how can you find your inner wisdom to guide you?

## My Purpose Is

When I start working with a client, we first create what I call a Map of Healing. In this Map of Healing, we talk, and I do all the writing. Life is one; life is all holistic. But to address it in a systematic way, we look at different areas one at a time—relationships, overall health and well-being, work/career/life purpose. Often, someone is okay in one area of their life, but wants help in another.

We look at what's going on in each of these areas. What challenges does the person face? But we don't just talk about the problem. We also discuss where they'd like to be. What would that look like, if they achieved what they wanted? How would that feel? What seems to be stopping them?

We start with that a Map of Healing because journaling and writing are such powerful tools. Many times, our minds are moving a mile a minute. We don't know what we want. Or we want one thing, but then something else gets our attention and we want something different. So we spend time being together in this space of just listening, and writing it out. That's the first step.

Then we really go into the many fears, worries, and beliefs that are in the way. I do a lot with clearing. I use a process called Levels of the Mind, based on the teachings of David Hoffmeister and A Course in Miracles. Basically, it's like looking at your mind from inside.

Imagine that you have a map of your mind and that you can go inside of it. If you could see where you are, then it would be much easier to negotiate. But often, people just don't know. They don't understand themselves. They're too busy with the daily outer pressures.

I use this tool called Levels of the Mind to understand your perceptions, your thoughts, your beliefs, your desires, and your fears. You really get to know yourself. And then you can make changes because knowledge is power.

Then I invite my clients to think about creativity in their lives. What do they enjoy? What brings them passion? What motivates them? What would they love to do, and how can they connect to that?

The other important piece of healing I share is connection-both social connection and connection to yourself. That's where the meditation and guided visualizations come in. Because before you can really enjoy happy, healthy, fulfilling, and prosperous relationships with others, you need to have a healthy relationship with yourself.

I would also add communication. Many people really struggle with expressing themselves. Communication enhances our ability to create and to connect.

## My Gift for You

My gift is a guided meditation. It's a tool to help you stop, be still, and come to that space of quiet—just being with yourself where you are. You don't have to do anything. You don't have to breathe a certain way or do anything complicated.

But sometimes we can't do that by ourselves, so you have me as your guide, holding that space for you to find stillness and let that stillness lead you. So when you're facing something external that's got you all wired and tired, this meditation helps you turn in, be quiet, be still, and access your inner resources.

Grab your gift from Dr. Seema Khaneja at: www.SuperwomanBook.com/gifts

## My Advice for You in Your Journey

As entrepreneurs, we're busy. We have many demands, many things we need to do. We want to do the best we can and to be of service. But the busier we are, usually the more we need to slow down.

So when you think you don't have a minute, that's where you need a lot of minutes. When you're feeling like you can't figure something out and you want to do more, take a moment to turn inward and simply stop and be.

It could be just a moment. It doesn't have to be a long time. But cultivate that habit of stopping. The answers aren't all "out there."

Think about when you search for something on the internet. You get bombarded with information. You have no idea what you need or what you want. And before you know it, you've got to move on to the next task. So, you carry that unfinished business with you.

But you can stop and say, "Okay, I'm going to be quiet. I'm going to take a walk, or I'm going to journal. I'm going to be quiet for a minute." You could even meet a friend for lunch or coffee, or just do something simple that would nurture you. Go inward. Be quiet.

In the end, you will save time. You will find that you're more productive, more energized, and more creative.

The way we experience
the world around us is a
direct reflection of the
world within us.

~ Gabrielle Bernstein

# FROM BURNOUT TO CLARITY
## I am alive & intending to thrive.

*Emerald GreenForest*

## My Superwoman Breakthrough

I didn't get close to burnout; I actually did burn out. In 2017 I came to a place in my business where I was trying all the things and I had been in the business for nearly a decade. I became really clear that it was no longer serving me to be doing business the way I was doing business. And I made a decision, December of 2016. I said to myself, I am taking six weeks off because if I don't, I'm going to die here.

It was not working the way it needed to work. I knew that if my business could not support me through the six-week period of time that I had, then I would have to make some new choices in my life.

When I came back online February 1, 2017, I gave myself until my birthday, which was February 18th. And I said to myself, it will tell me, I will see whether I'm going in the right direction with this or not.

So I did all the things. I got myself geared back up again. I made some affiliate calls and promoted partners. I went out and networked. I did all the things that you do when you're in business that are intended to move things in a positive, profitable direction.

By my birthday I had made $7. And this was after having generated multiple millions of dollars over several years in this business.

It was a pretty clear sign to me that doing business that way was complete. I decided to literally have a fire and I threw everything into the fire and said, okay, I surrender. So that's what I did.

I actually had a fire ceremony at the beginning of March 2017. Then I had to surrender even more and just give my business, financial security, my life path and everything else up to spirit.

I said, okay, I give it up to you, show me what to do. And I sat.

I sat for ten days. During that time, it was frustrating when you're used to moving things forward.

Well, I moved myself into oblivion essentially and so I was in that dynamic of "keep on moving". Then I had to do what I call stop the world and drain the momentum out of forward motion in the wrong direction.

I was sitting there thinking, okay, so there's a mortgage payment that's due, how are we going to make that happen?

The inspiration that came through initially was to make sales. It's a skill, so I was able to look at my own skill set, because I can do sales, and even high-ticket sales. That led me to put myself out there to do high ticket sales.

And then the miracle happened several days after that, on 17th of March. Now I was seventeen days into the month of March surrendering and putting myself out there to do sales and I was selected to be a case study on a TV show called Fix My Brand.

It came out of some of the networking I had done in February when I was trying to generate things again. I reached back into my past and reconnected with someone I hadn't talked to since 2010. And she had just been selected to produce this TV show by Apple TV.

We reconnected and I was selected to be a case study and during the fix my brand process, a whole new brand came along with a whole new audience.

I was guided in that process to begin serving men more than women. And that's not to say that my door is not open to women. What's interesting is when I started to serve men and I created my Men On Purpose Podcast, (which is now being heard in fifty-six countries around the world, downloaded thousands of times around the world) we just keep growing in momentum.

It has been a beautiful, consistent upward trend. It's systematized and it's just like all the things that you know you want to have in your business including that it's monetized. As I started to put that into play and create success with it, women started knocking on my backdoor.

For ten years I served mostly women and I helped them feel great speaking and powerful asking for money. Now I serve mostly men, but women are knocking on the back door and I have both women and men clients. It's fascinating what happens when you surrender, and how things come that you weren't expecting. And then the job really is to say yes. So when the men came in, I was like, really? I'm supposed to be serving men? This is interesting.

But I said yes, I'll do it. I got clear that the best way for marketing men was a podcast format and I love my podcast. I love, love, love my podcast because it's a great business card. It gets attention and because I'm a woman doing a podcast called Men On Purpose, I automatically have a curiosity factor.

The other thing I like about this style of business that it's not about me now. It's about them. I'm really focusing my energy, attention and intention on elevating, celebrating, and spotlighting men on purpose.

There are some days, where I don't feel like getting dressed up and looking like I should on my Instagram. There are some days where it's just like, enough is enough and I want to just go crawl into a hole and cuddle with my cat somewhere.

Sometimes a personality-based business brand, you really have to live into that on a constant basis. For me, this is being more about service to them than it is about elevating me. I'm just coming along for the ride even though I'm doing the work.

## My Tools & Rituals to Stay in the Flow

I think the main thing is the whole idea of stopping the world. Stopping the world is a process that I actually learned many years ago when I first became initiated in the shamanic path. It's something that we don't really think about when we are thinking about either starting or growing our business.

But if you think about it, your world has certain touch points that keep you in place. If you would imagine a table that's set where the salt and pepper is here, and the napkins are over there, and the forks are over here, and the cups are over there. It's like a setting and you are in the setting. And it just keeps playing over and over again as long as you stay in that setting and the momentum for keeping things the same becomes very, very strong.

When you stop the world and literally clear the table, which is what I did with a fire ceremony, I cleared the table and I offered up everything that was on that table. All my business cards, my little peacock themed brand including a peacock puppet, went in. All my mind maps went in the fire, and all my old programs went in—everything went in the fire.

Fire ceremony is my second powerful practice. It includes that process of stopping the world and literally clearing the slate so that you can free yourself from momentum that's no longer serving and then have the stillness to open for that next inspiration.

And then the third ritual for me is once I've cleared the space, is becoming incredibly intentional about what I want next.

One major intention when I went through the fix my brand process was to keep things simple. If it's not simple, I'm not doing it. I am done with complexity. I am so complete with complexity.

I set the intention right from the beginning with this new business model. It has got to be simple, simple, simple. And the hardest thing for me was detaching my own neurology from the old way, which was beginning to be run on fear rather than running on my clear intention, passion and desire.

The biggest challenge was getting the healing I needed to extract myself physically, mentally, emotionally, and spiritually from the old patterns. The third piece of my ritual involved getting help from medicine women, from colleagues, and asking for help to reframe and reset my life in a way that is meaningful, purposeful, powerful, profitable, playful, pleasurable, all the P's.

And then I learned to be honest with myself when I have that tendency to want to go back into that old way and make a shift.

## My Purpose Is

I think one of the greatest gifts that I offer is my capacity to see really clearly. I can see the bigger picture that other people might have an inkling of, but they don't have the whole thing.

For example, I was on the phone today with a man who's at the end of his long-term career with a very big corporation. And He has also gone through this huge cancer journey with twenty-five cancer treatments and surgeries

We were on the phone together and he says, "well, I really feel like I want to inspire people, but I don't know if this is worthwhile. He has zero idea of how to set himself up or how to value his experience & life story properly so that he can be beautifully compensated for sharing his journey. I can provide vision for somebody and I can help them to craft their legacy, which in his case will be legendary if he's able to make the decision to say YES to his calling.

I can help people to craft their legacy in a way that is powerful, potent, and profitable. Clarity is my greatest gift of all, when I serve people, I help them to become clear.

When I first started down this path of being in this space of online entrepreneurship and personal and professional development, the main comment that I would get back from people after we'd worked together was, "I feel so much lighter." They would feel so much lighter.

Another gift of mine when people hire me to work with them as their mentor to help them literally strip away everything that's in the way of them becoming who they are meant to be. I am a perfect example of stripping away everything that's in the way because I do it again and again and again myself. I call that serpent medicine, where I'm helping them to shed their "old skin" so that they can be renewed and grow into the next greatest expression of who they are and present that to the world.

I have a lot of gifts and that is another ritual I had to do last year as part of my healing, to actually acknowledge my own gifts. I went through a huge process with my medicine bundle where I inventoried my gifts from a very objective point of view. I then anchored those gifts into a particular stone in my medicine bundle, so that I can continually go back to remembering that I have gifts and appreciating and valuing them.

I think a lot of times what people do is they undervalue their own gifts and they overvalue what other people are doing. They often think what if what somebody else is doing is better than what they have to offer. In fact, the things that come easiest for you are generally your most valuable gifts to other people.

Envying somebody else or their gifts does two things that don't serve you. First of all, it's disrespectful to the gifts that you have of your own. Secondly, whenever you envy somebody else, you've got to take their Karma on as well. If you want what they have for gifts, you have got to go through whatever they went through and you don't know what that might be.

Overall, it's important not to envy other people of their gifts, but to celebrate the gifts of others so that we can collaborate and come together. We can pool our gifts and make one plus one equal eleven.

## My Gift for You

My gift is the Instant Clarity Exercise. I've created this 8-minute audio because I think especially for entrepreneurs, one of the biggest challenges we have is being faced with hundreds of small and large decisions daily.

Should I invest here? Well, if I do this, is it going to equal that? How are we going to get from here to there? Decisions, decisions, decisions. Should I set up an LLC? What are my tax consequences? How am I going to get clients? What's my message?

There are all of these decisions that we have to make, and we've got to be, as entrepreneurs, swift and sure. It's important to be swift and sure in our decision making, even in places where we don't know where we're going, and we want to be able to make the clearest decision possible.

A lot of people get stuck in confusion and they don't do anything. Then they're like a whirling tornado of ideas and possibilities and they're standing still. If you ever saw a tornado standing still, it's creating a lot of destruction. It is not creating anything positive other than cleansing the land where its stationary over it.

The Instant Clarity Exercise will help to make the decision-making process exponentially easier. I take you through a process where if you're facing some major decisions, by the time you're done with the eight minutes, you will know what you're going to do. You will have your decision.

Grab your gift from Emerald GreenForest at:
www.SuperwomanBook.com/gifts

## My Advice for You in Your Journey

I'll give you my Five "I's" of The Wise. The first I is Take
Inspired action. So when you're inspired, take the action. Say
Yes. Like what happened with the men and help them be more
on purpose. I was just like really men? Yes. I was inspired. Say
yes to inspiration. That usually means you need to Invest which
is the second "I" of the wise. I've invested a lot of time, energy
and money in building my new business and my new brand.

The third "I" of the why's is to Immerse yourself. When
you're working with somebody like Maribel or myself or any
of the other co-authors in this book—you've made the
inspired action, the investment, and then you immerse yourself
in whatever it is that your mentors, trainers or coaches are
guiding you to do.

Then Integrate what you're learning. Sometimes when we
integrate, we have to throw out things that we used to think.
We have to throw out old mindsets, old patterns of behavior,
old beliefs to integrate the new that we are receiving from a
higher point of view.

And then finally the fifth "I" of the wise is Implement. All
of this is great, but if you aren't implementing, nothing's
happening. To summarize, my advice is to take Inspired action,
Invest, Immerse, Integrate and Implement. This is the wisest
way to convert your wisdom into wealth!

Sometimes when we
integrate, we have to
throw out things that we
used to think.

~ Emerald GreenForest

# FROM TRAGEDY TO WRITING A NEW STORY
## I am my story.

*Michele Gunderson*

## My Superwoman Breakthrough

I've found that what's happening in my business is so connected with what's happening in my life. And If you're talking about overwhelm, this was certainly the most overwhelming crazy week of my life.

It started when I got a note from my daughter's school that said there was somebody who was threatening to use a gun at her school.

I was getting ready to teach a week-long retreat, doing everything, and all of a sudden that paled in comparison. And then what do you do?

The floor just fell out from under me. Will my daughter be safe?

She was supposed to show up at school the next day for a final exam. Late that night she was on the phone with her best friend, and I was on the phone with my man, Shelley.

Do I let my daughter go to school? Do I hold her back and make her stay home? What if the threat is real?

My man—he was my support, my rock that night.

"It's going to be okay," he said. I could feel his arms around me, holding me, so I could figure out what to do.

When my daughter was off the phone, she was clear: "Mom, I need to go. My friends will be there. I need to write these exams. I have to be with my friends."

So I let her go. I watched my daughter walk into the school that day, and I didn't know if she was going to walk out alive.

I talked to my man, of course, right after I watched her walk into the school. I kept talking to him as he calmed me down. It's going to be okay, he said. All the while, the police cars circled the school.

As entrepreneurs, we have so much stuff going on, but what happens at home matters. It's everything. That day, all I wanted was for my daughter to come home safely that night.

And she did. She came home. Everything was going to be okay.

The next day, the phone rang, and it was from Texas where my man was. I picked up the phone, "Hey, Shelley," I said, looking forward to his calm voice, his soothing presence.

The voice on the other end of the line was a woman's. Flat voice. Something was wrong, terribly wrong.

"This isn't Shelley, it's Shelley's mom," the voice said. "Shelley is dead."

Sometimes we get blindsided, so focused on one thing when all of a sudden, something else comes rushing into our lives. It was from out of nowhere.

My man was healthy. He drank kale smoothies for breakfast. He trained folks at the gym, cycled for hours, stayed fit and strong. He could do pushups with one arm or with the weight of a person on top of him. Once, he ran down the beach in Mexico with me on his shoulders, both of us laughing. He was forty-eight years old. Then suddenly he was gone.

I picked up the phone and called my friend Sarah. It was minutes after I'd heard the news. What do you say?

Sarah listened as I told her I had to leave to teach a week-long retreat in two days. Of course, she said you can't go. Let's figure out what to do. But I knew what I wanted, even then.

"Sarah, I'm going. I need to go. These people are flying in from everywhere. They're counting on me." I knew I had to be there.

More craziness out of nowhere, this time little details of things to organize in a sea of overwhelm and grief. My washing machine broke down; I couldn't even clean clothes for my daughter. My visa was stolen, so I had to go to the bank to sort it out. I even needed to buy a car, of all things, to drive out to the mountains to get to the retreat—it had been arranged the week before, and my old vehicle wouldn't make it out through the mountain roads.

When we got to the retreat center, I turned on the music and danced with my students. We started our week together dancing, just dancing. The words of the song echoed through the room: "The rest is still unwritten..." It was powerful. I knew it would be the best retreat I'd ever taught.

So what's the next page in the story?

Here's what I knew: even though it felt like the end, I was still in the middle of the story. My story. My students' stories.

It wasn't the end.

I'll never forget that dance with my students. They were all grieving. It was like our hearts had been yanked out of our chests—some of them cried all day when they heard the news. But the dance was amazing.

People often ask me how I did it. How did you keep functioning? How did you keep going? What made you so strong?

I've been working with words and stories for over twenty-five years, and what I learned so deeply in that week is this: the things I've been teaching about story, they're real. They matter.

It's always been about creating an empowering story for yourself and your company. Stories matter.

But you have to know where you are in the story. And you can turn the page and engage in a different story. The story that I was engaged in was that my students needed me. I promised them I'd be there. So I was there.

## My Tools & Rituals to Stay in the Flow

It's exactly the things that I teach my students: stories are everywhere. I remember that on a daily basis.

My daughter was in the midst of her own story about what mattered, and I wanted to honor that.

Your team is in the midst of their own story, as are your clients and vendors and joint venture partners. We have stories when we're dancing or crying, when we're brushing our teeth or speaking or handing details in the midst of a launch. We're in a story when we're running our businesses each moment of each day. We create stories all the time about how we think it is going to go or how it's not going to go. And that changes everything.

Stories are everywhere. When I remember that, I can see where I am in the story.

There are empowering stories and there are disempowering stories. It's important to know the difference.

I always try to remember, moment by moment, that I can choose the story I engage in.

What's the story I'm living? What's the story I'm telling the world?

Those are the tools that have been teaching and working with and living for over twenty-five years. That's what makes a profound difference for me and for my clients.

## My Purpose Is

I help entrepreneurs tell better stories so they can grow their business, lead happier lives, and have a lot more joyful moments no matter what is happening in their businesses and their lives. My clients go from having less impact than what they're capable of, to creating five- or six-figure months easily in a business they love.

## My Gift for You

I have a resource called Anatomy Of An Empowering Story. It explains what the biggest story mistake is that most entrepreneurs make, and what to do about it. It provides examples of empowering stories and gives entrepreneurs concrete steps they can take right now to start to live an empowering story, both in their businesses and their lives. I used to think I couldn't share this knowledge with those I hadn't met and worked closely with—I had a disempowering story myself!

It took me years to understand that I could do it—I could get the essence of this powerful story wisdom across in just a few pages. I created this powerful resource for others to find their own empowering story, to help them catapult to the next level in their businesses and their lives.

Grab your gift from Michele Gunderson at: www.SuperwomanBook.com/gifts

## My Advice for You in Your Journey

Your Life is your story. Which story do you want to choose? Your story matters.

Choose wisely for yourself so you can be playful and prosperous. Learn about story so you can really create the life and the company you love.

Your Life is your story.
Which story do you want
to choose?

~ Michele Gunderson

# THE NEW MODEL OF SELLING WAS BORN
## I am abundant.

*Jennifer Diepstraten*

## My Superwoman Breakthrough

I was ten years into my job in corporate sales, working in a biotech company selling microscopes to research scientists. I had a great six-figure income, with all the bells and whistles: company credit card, medical insurance, car allowance. I even had a Staples charge card.

Then one morning, things shift. I'm in my black pants, low-heeled boots, and modest "I'm going to talk to scientists" dressy t-shirt. At the time, my husband was home taking care of our two sons. He had basically retired from home construction right after the real estate crash. I come around the corner and there's my husband and two kids, eight in the morning on a workday, sitting on the couch giggling. Playing

tickle. The shrieks of joy, seeing the three of them together...
pierces my awareness. In that moment, I lose my temper.

Yes, sure, I was thankful for the opportunity we had for my
husband to be home with the kids. It was my choice to
continue working and not be a stay-at-home parent. I rarely
saw my boss and seldom had to report to an office. I even liked
my customers and had plenty of time for family. But somehow,
that job was just not enough.

I'll tell you, there was this thing that had been bubbling up
for many years; there was more that I could do. A bigger
impact to make.

And even though I had tried to make my job into
something that was deeply fulfilling, I always felt under-
utilized. Boxed in. There was also definitely a lid to how much
I could make at work even though I was doing very well. There
was more that I wanted to contribute and earn.

That morning, I said a few things that I am not proud of. I
guess my words woke us all up to the fact that it was time for
Mom to make a change.

Later I remember sitting and talking to my oldest son who
was ten at the time. I said to him, "You know, Dylan, I've got
this opportunity to either keep doing what I've been doing at
work, which earns good money. Or I can go do this other thing
that I've been dreaming about. I don't know what's going to
happen if I follow that route. I don't know how the money's
going to turn out. I just know that it's something in my heart
that I really want to do."

"What should I do?" I said to him.

He said simply, "Mom, I think you should follow your
heart."

So I resigned from my job. It was funny because after I left,
I told my son that I had quit and he looked at me with these
big round eyes and said, "Mom, I hope it works!" Me too,
buddy.

Then I started on my own adventure as an entrepreneur and
that's where I am today.

It worked.

## My Tools & Rituals to Stay in the Flow

It's so important to get your support team in place. That means getting support in your home and with your business.

I have an amazing husband and kids that fully support what we're doing with our business because they understand. We've included them as part of our process.

That support doesn't have to be a spouse, it could be a sister or a mom or a cousin or a friend, but somebody that you feel has your back. I'm sure that I could not have done what I've done without that.

I think there's a common misconception for a lot of people that a relationship will take time away from building your business or from what it is that you want. I've heard from a lot of women that think they should build their business first and then they can have their ideal relationship.

I believe that a great partnership actually fuels the business and a great business choice fuels your relationship. It actually adds to your life, it doesn't take away from it. Being an entrepreneur can be hard, and when I'm about to take a big risk and my own courage is all used up, I borrow my husband's courage. He's my rock.

One of my rituals is to tend to my relationship, like having a regular date night with my husband. We prioritize our time with the family and make sure we are all present by doing things like having no phones at the dinner table.

Also, my husband and I go for a beach walk and talk once a week as part of our business. We talk about what want to do and the things that we're excited about. It's the place where we get to unpack new ideas and unravel challenges, away from the daily demands of business.

Other things that I do to make sure that I'm filled up and fueled? Take my dog and kids on a nature walk. I love to spend time outdoors. I listen to some of my favorite inspirational audios when I walk. Take long Epsom salt baths. Work out regularly. I also enjoy meditating and I eat really healthy to support my body and feel my best all day.

## My Purpose Is

I help coaches, consultants, and service-based business owners get great at sales. Our sales transformation courses allow entrepreneurs to be fully aligned when selling so they don't have to pretend to be someone else or say inauthentic things to make sales. They realize that sales IS service. Our clients easily raise their fees, gain confidence, and find the words make big sales with ease.

I had over fifteen years of sales experience and sold multiple millions of dollars in my previous jobs, so I had that going for me when I started my business with my husband. We tapped into that strength and started our business we have now, which is called High Ticket Sales Success. We serve people in person and virtually all over North America and Europe.

I love what I do because I feel like I'm creating a whole army of people who are out to make a difference. I love helping them to be successful because as a result, they get paid really well for what they do, and they can continue to do more of it.

## My Gift for You

The old model of selling really is dead or dying. What I mean by that is that so many of us have been taught that we have to "drive for the close," overcome the objections, and make the sale. That was the kind of attitude that I grew up in when I was in corporate sales and it's still prevalent. It's on its way out because today's consumer is far too savvy to be taken in.

When so many of our clients start with us, they've been to that kind of sales training. They've gotten a sales script and they're just not able to make it work for them. They often feel like they're working against themselves. If you're in the business to help someone or heal someone or coach someone, how can you take something from them? How can you start your relationship by taking or manipulating them into buying from you? If sales feels like that to you, even a little bit, it's never going to work.

Thus, I created a downloadable book for entrepreneurs, the business people really striving to make a difference, called The High Ticket Selling Revolution.

In it, I teach how to have conversations that empower people to move forward, serve them, and create a win-win through a sale if they're a fit for your offer. As someone whose main desire is to help people, it's important to create a balance of giving and selling because you don't want to err on the side of giving everything away; you have to sell to stay in business. There's a flow and rhythm to giving and receiving. In the book, I've included the 9 Secrets to Increase Your Fees, Convert More Sales, and Magnetically Attract Top Dollar Clients. There's even a formula for how to quadruple your income within four months without selling out or feeling pushy.

Grab your gift from Jennifer Diepstraten at: www.SuperwomanBook.com/gifts

## My Advice for You in Your Journey

You really can have whatever you want. Truly. I've noticed that everything we do works to some degree or another. Even your so-called failures are working for you. So you've got to try things as fast as possible and not worry about failing. When you believe you can have whatever you want, then it just becomes a matter of choosing the stuff you really, really want.

One of my favorite sayings is, "The more fun I have, the more money I make." I believe you can choose your beliefs, and this is one that I've installed in my own thoughts. I just like it better than the alternative. Set your intention and then look for evidence to make those things become real. It all begins with you.

The more fun I have, the more money I make.

~ Jennifer Diepstraten

# FROM LIFE SUPPORT TO A NEW ME
## I am blessed.

*Suzi Picaso*

## My Superwoman Breakthrough

I'm ready to highlight a very personal part of my life that was a huge breakthrough for me. Some people may look at it as a time where they could have just given up, but for me, I took it as this is the time to shift into a new me without giving up.

To give you a little background, I am the youngest of ten children. I remember when I was seven years old, I had my first business doing makeup. I would charge my friends a penny to do their makeup. I remember that I always had that drive in me to create what I wanted.

Fast forward to my dream of becoming a celebrity makeup artist and helping people be their most beautiful self, from the inside out. I realized what I wanted to do and I started out as a makeup artist for thirteen years in the industry. Then I moved on to work as a youth coordinator, and then marketing and put my all into everything I did.

All along while I was on this journey doing everything and juggling my roles, I always felt like I had it together and from the outside, everyone looked at me as if I did.

However, I was an alcoholic and I had to come to terms with that. The way I finally recognized that I had a drinking problem was when I overdosed on Ambien® and vodka cranberry, which was my favorite drink.

I thought it was just a great social drink, but I just kept drinking and drinking them until I couldn't drink anymore. Then I overdosed, and it was the scariest night of my life.

I had recently gone through a second divorce and was out with friends. I remember looking around the room at everyone and seeing how happy they were in their relationships. Here I was getting ready to go to my condo and be by myself. When I entered my house, I thought to myself, here I am, this successful woman doing everything right but feeling so overwhelmed.

So I just made myself another drink and I emptied my purse to find that bottle of Ambien®. I took at least fifteen pills and soon after called my ex-husband, Joe and told him what I did. He immediately called 911 and an ambulance came to pick me up. I ended up on life support for the next five days.

While I was on life support, I had my mom, children, and friends that had been with me from the beginning all standing around me telling everyone this is it for me. I probably wouldn't make it.

When I came through on the fifth day, I woke up to my friend Carol, in my ear yelling at me saying, Suzi, you have so much more to give! Look at your daughters, look at your mom, they can't see you go this way. And she said, if you don't wake up, I don't know what I'll do without you, please wake up. Please wake up, your daughters need you, your mom needs you, you have so much more to give!

That's when I woke up and tried to pull out the tube they had in my throat to help me breathe. I couldn't do it because they had tied down my arms since I kept trying to rip it out. When I woke up and started to regroup, I thought, "What am I doing? Why would I do this?"

Then I shifted all my energy and mindset to how grateful and blessed I was to come through after five days. It was really shocking to the doctors and it was such a blessing because I had so many people standing around me praying for me and I know that's what did it.

From that point forward, I just started putting in place everything that I wanted to do. I wanted to someday have my own store and launch my own cosmetic line.

Within six months of me being on life support, I was able to open my store. Then nine months after that I launched my own cosmetic line called SuziQ Cosmetics. Within that time period, I had done makeup on over 400 celebrities in Hollywood.

I was able to shift all my negative energy and everything that I had taken for granted and focus it on how blessed I was and just go out there and do what I loved.

All of this happened by just shifting my mindset from, "Oh, look at me, I'm so sad I don't have anyone to believe in me, to believing that I could do anything."

I set my mindset to let go of all the negative thoughts because I was just making up all those stories in my head and thinking of the worst-case scenario. When I shifted to what I wanted instead of what I didn't want, that's when my whole life changed for the better.

## My Tools & Rituals to Stay in the Flow

Of course, I omitted alcohol and I started to take better care of myself by eating clean and exercising. I learned to say no. I had to realize that I couldn't say yes to everything because while I was opening my store, I had just been appointed to the city council.

Two months later I was running for president of the chamber and I got it. Then I realized I had a full plate, not just those two roles, but I was also a business owner of my new company. I realized it is now time to start saying no.

That was hard for me because I've always been a yes person. Anytime I could help, I would say yes. I recognized how quickly I was depleting all my energy by saying yes so much and that had to stop.

In doing all the things to take care of myself like working out, eating clean, not drinking alcohol, and instead drinking a lot of water, learning to say no, and growing my faith, I was able to get off of Synthroid® which I was on for ten years.

My life just changed so dramatically. I had so many blessings that were surrounding me and I had to become aware and grateful. I think without the alcohol beginning to see my life so clearly now, I could see who my true friends were. I began to see the light that I had before, there was just a little flicker. Fortunately, that little flicker turned into a flame that helped guide me to go in the right direction.

## My Purpose Is

I work with college students that are at risk. They enter a program in their career choice and it begins with me, teaching them strategies for success including emotional intelligence, how to create affirmations and block out what I call "negative wizards". I call them negative wizards because those are the people that come around us and say that you can't do this or you're not from this background so you can't do that.

I also volunteer in the community. I share as much as I can on different platforms to women and college students, to let them know that they can enter any room without armor, and they don't need to have a title to be a leader. I learned that to be successful it starts with your beliefs. I would enter a room with just believing in myself, knowing what I had to offer and if someone gave me the chance, I would prove myself to them.

Anyone can do that, and that's what I continue to share with others to inspire them to create the life they want.

## My Gift for You

My gift is called, The Mindset of a Winner. It's a series to show you how to shift your mindset from focusing on the past and what you think is wrong or your mistakes, to what is possible for you. When you do that, you open up all the possibilities that are going to lead you to your greatest self.

If you are struggling in your life with addiction, and overall unhappy, I want to help you change your life in a positive way. I want to show you how I did it because I'm passionate about helping others create their best life.

Grab your gift from Suzi Picaso at: www.SuperwomanBook.com/gifts

## My Advice for You in Your Journey

Believe in yourself. Don't waste your energy by holding on to an invisible backpack full of all the things that you did wrong. I encourage you to look forward and live in the moment because you can't change anything from the past.

Today is an opportunity to be your best. Surround yourself with a circle of people with light who will support you and not try to tear you down. When you have a strong network of women who can support each other, then you can do anything. You can begin again and look for opportunities all around you every day. Create the life you want now.

Don't waste your energy
by holding on to an
invisible backpack full of
all the things that you
did wrong.

~ Suzi Picaso

# TURNING THE SHIP TO
# FIND MY PURPOSE
I am a connector.

*Ginger Johnson*

## My Superwoman Breakthrough

Envision a really, really large ship on the ocean: enormous, aircraft carriers, big huge tankers, freighters. And think of that as your life and then you think, "oh, wait a minute. I was going there. Now, I want to go there." That was me about two and a half years ago. I'd been in my own business for upwards of fifteen or sixteen years at that point. I'd created different businesses from scratch, businesses that nobody else on the planet has done.

Two and a half years ago I found myself on that ship thinking, "You know what, I'm not going that way anymore. Where is the ship going to go?"

I was in a serious soul-searching mode and stage. I wasn't leaving something because I wanted to leave it. I was leaving it because I needed to make more traction. I wanted to have a way bigger impact and I wanted to reach toward an audience that really wanted that impact. It was easy for me to say, "okay, it's time to change," because I'd done that before. Then it was, "alright, if I'm going to change, then what does that look like?"

That's when you start to turn the ship. Turning a ship is not a quick maneuver. You've got to have all the gear you need. You need to ask the right people, and you've got to start connecting in different ways. The very first thing you connect with is your Why. Such as, "Why do I want to turn the ship?" To begin with: "Where do I think I want to go?" That was the biggest question for me.

I didn't know where I wanted to go, so I had to figure that out. It felt like the ship spun in a few cookies at first. And it was really invigorating to give myself the permission to say, "You know what? It's not going to be that thing and I'm okay with that. That's good. I feel really proud of that, but I'm going to put that on the back burner."

Then, to help figure out where we were going, I did what I called 'prairie dogging', it's a good visual. I'm thinking, okay, what do I want to do?

Whatever we want to do, ask yourself, "What do I want to do?" And interestingly enough, I don't necessarily think, "What do I know the most about or what do I feel the most confident about or where do I have the most experience?"

For me, it's coming from my gut and my heart together. They're talking to each other and we want to do something that we really find rewarding. That's fun!

That's what makes life playful, prosperous and peaceful. Truly. So, I would pop out of the ground. "Oh, oh, I'm going to do this, this is what it's going to be!" (that's prairie dogging).

And then, I'd start going back underground. Again, I'd pop up. I probably did it three or four times and each time it was something different because I love the volcano part of the idea.

Once that prairie dog (me) shot out of the earth, I'd think, "Oh well wait a minute… let's think about this a little bit more."

I gave myself the permission to brainstorm very freely every single day because I have trained myself how to do it. I know that when the juices are flowing, that's the best time to really be thinking out loud and giving myself permission. Get rid of any boundaries, any parameters, and just say: I need to think and thinking is the whole goal here. It's not a wasted errand. It's never a waste of time so I gave myself that opportunity and latitude to think in that time.

I started investing in myself again, seriously, for the first time since college. In this case that meant I started looking around for expert advice. I started looking at and asking people who I liked and trusted and knew were successful in their own right. Asking them what they did for their own professional development?

It turned out that it's all about professional and personal development. I began attending events and meeting others who changed my life for the better.

When you're turning your ship, one of the biggest takeaways I want to share with people who want to be superwoman in their own right and have their own definition, is please know that investing in yourself wisely is always worth every single penny.

You've got to believe that there will always be more money, because there always will be. There will never be more you. If you're going to turn your ship in any way, shape or form, maybe you have a dinghy or a raft, maybe you have a supertanker, whatever it is, invest in yourself.

By prairie dogging, I certainly invested in myself and started showing up, building new cohorts, and meeting truly remarkable people. I needed to get out of the world I had been in. And the only way you do that is to do it is physically. For me, the best way is to physically go and do something. It meant showing up at different things and being present to making connections.

The ship started to turn and I still didn't know where it was going. I didn't know where the compass was headed. I just knew it was progress because I felt differently. I felt more invigorated in a positive way.

And so again, in turning that ship—prairie dogging—I started to reach out. Who's that over there and what are they doing over there? And maybe if I stand on a chair in the back of the room and say this, I'll actually do something! Since I'm a doer, I just needed to do in different ways.

Finally on one of those prairie dog pop ups, I realize, "Oh my gosh—it's connectivity!!" with the lightning bolt and the birds singing in the clouds. That's what I've been doing all along. Nobody I know or have heard of is a connectivity expert. Maybe there is somebody out there doing this work, but I haven't found anyone who's put their stake in the ground and made it their mission to show others the power of connectivity.

Always be confident that if you believe in something enough, if you believe in yourself enough, you can believe in something that you can do enough. That is one of your true superpowers.

Don't let anybody else cloud your vision because they're not you. So while people sharing advice are usually well-intended, they're still not you. They're still not going to live your life and do the work that you want to do. If you can see that vision, you can make it happen.

I've started a pillow company. I've studied women and their relationship with beer and now I'm becoming a connectivity expert and it's so much fun!

Right now I'm deep into the science and I'm learning what my science is so I'm an expert in my own way. And I'm going to become so much better with my expertise that the shift now is just going full speed ahead and I'm not sure which area it's going to! All the same, it's going into water that I want to be in. I'll find the right people and the right people will resonate and I'll learn. It's this incredibly elastic wonderland of it all coming together.

The biggest part of my story and the one I'm absolutely the most excited about is that I've found my passion and purpose that fits me.

It took me a lot longer than I wanted it to, but I realize that investing in myself, and giving myself permission is what was necessary. Education isn't cheap and we need to weigh the dollar amount of investment, just like any kind of degree. It's worth it if you're going to apply it. You're really investing in yourself. Find those programs and people and courses and coaches and whoever they are. Vet them carefully and then invest in yourself. You're going to be so glad you did. It'll help you turn your ship better, more accurately, and you'll have a whole bunch of new cohorts who can share your vision.

## My Tools & Rituals to Stay in the Flow

First of all, the grind culture is not a healthy culture; focus on peace. We'll hit that one first because it's the first one in your trifecta. Peaceful to me starts with your own peace first. It took me a long time to understand the value, for example, of meditation. I've always enjoyed quiet time for solitude, or whatever you want to call it. I've never felt alone and that I need time by myself.

Peacefulness to me is building a routine and a routine isn't boring. A routine is a framework and a foundation. For instance, I had trouble sleeping for years. I used to be able to stand sleeping up in the corner as a kid and I lost that. And that affects everything! I started doing research on sleep. You know, it's not something we can assume that we know how to do all the time. Our bodies change as we age. And so those things changed. I started reading and learning. Now, I'm sleeping better than I have in more than a decade. It's been a game changer. My attitude, my mindset and everything is different because of that. I'm better for my clients. I'm better for me and I'm more creative. All these things are peaceful. I tap into them.

I'm also taking a really close look at who are my closest friends. Even though I love having a lot of friends and I love knowing a lot of people because there's so much value, I've taken a look at the different ripples, as I call them. Who's going to be with me in the long haul, with the intensity that I can lean on; who can give that back? I have a good girlfriend who is a lawyer. If that isn't an intense profession, I don't know what is! When I saw her the other day, I told her I'm going into this stage and I'm really focusing in. I told her, "I need you to be there for me, will you?"

And she said, "Absolutely yes."

That doesn't just happen. You have to be strategic about that and careful. Your friends will change. You'll shed some and that's okay. So being peaceful is also accepting that. Taking a look at that doesn't mean you dismiss them. It simply means that you shift what your interactions are.

I have a fabulous husband who I adore, and two great four-legged kids, and we play and do a lot together. We host a lot of dinner parties since we like the entertainment and hospitality value of having people come together in our home and taking care of them. It's just so much dang fun and not many people do it, so it's extra special. We have a lot of laughter in our household, which is memorable. Laughter is truly contagious and it's good for our health along with other benefits.

Smile more, do whatever kinds of things promote the playfulness in you and prosperity comes. Money isn't all prosperity by a long shot. Yet in the way that prosperity means money, you have to have faith. I don't believe in hope, but I do believe in faith.

Faith to me is being in front of the lake and saying, "I'm going to get across" and you figure it out. You get a ride, you scuba, you walk around, you take a plane—it doesn't matter. Hope is waiting for somebody else to come pick you up. I wouldn't put hope in the business arena or success arena. Hope is like luck.

Faith is belief, conviction and attraction. For prosperity, you have to have an unshakeable belief. Be around people who also understand prosperity.

When you really put your value stake in the ground, that shifts everything because as soon as we shift our own value stake—that we know we're worth it—then that changes everything.

## My Purpose Is

I help people understand the power of Connectivity. It involves asking some critical questions. Critical is a good thing and involves critiquing, examining, and evaluating, so you gain solid clarity. There are so many other things about connectivity, which is why I wrote the book—the Creativity Canon and teach the Connectivity Framework.

## My Gift for You

My gift is the Connectivity Framework. I outlined the seven Elements to help people understand the power of connection. Connectivity is connecting with people on purpose with a service mindset. I'm really, really clear on what my intention is and that guides everything. I think one of the most powerful things about clarity, is that we learn to tune out what doesn't fit. It's not just about focusing on what does fit. It's about letting go and putting on hold the stuff that doesn't, and you're magnetizing everything that does match up. It brings speed. The Connectivity Framework is a structure that supports all of this clarity, that connection to self and connection to others.

Grab your gift from Ginger Johnson at: www.SuperwomanBook.com/gifts

# My Advice for You in Your Journey

I'll close it out with three things, because three is a magic number for lots of things. First of all, decide your "why". I constantly circle back to that. Your "why" is your guide. Figure that out. Invest your time in figuring out what that is. Give yourself the leeway, flexibility and understanding that sometimes it takes a little bit longer. If you can get there, then that's half the battle.

Number two is be really clear. Be really clear on what you're going to do and what you're not going to do, because I know that when I was turning my ship, it would be and was very easy for me to slip back into that old direction because it was familiar. But familiar doesn't mean that it's comfortable and it doesn't mean that it's the right direction.

And number three is to have fun. One of my mantras is, "Have fun or get out," because life is too short. We never get more time and there's always more opportunity for people who have fun.

*Have fun or get out.*

~ *Ginger Johnson*

# FROM BROKENNESS TO BREAKTHROUGH
## I am loved. I am happy.

## Stacey Lievens

**My Superwoman Breakthrough**

2018 was a magical year for me. But before the magic happened, I was at the lowest part of my entire life.

I was coming off a recent breakup of my twenty-three-year relationship with my ex-husband, Daniel. It was very painful. I had a lot of dark nights of the soul. In fact, I got so down and lost, that I ended up in the hospital. I thought I had a heart attack. The doctors decided to keep me overnight and perform an angiogram in the morning.

Needless to say, I was very scared. I remember lying in the ICU at two o'clock in the morning with wires coming up both of my arms, crying. I said "God, what are you trying to tell me?"

I felt broken.

In that moment, I remembered that a dear friend of mine, Lisa Sasevich, had suggested a few months earlier that I sign up for a program called HeartCore Leadership. I didn't know what I was signing up for, but I did it anyway because one of my best friends in the world said, "Stacey, I love you. Trust me. Sign up for this leadership course."

The course would start on June 11th, and I was laying in ICU at the end of May. I cried and prayed, "God, just get me to this leadership course. I think I'll have my answers there."

I had an angiogram the next morning, even though I actually felt healthy again by that time. The doctors told me that I hadn't had a heart attack. They called it a stress-related cardiac event.

I realized my body was talking to me, hitting me over the head with a two-by-four to wake me up. I said to myself, "Stop being a victim. Get up, move forward, and change your life."

That moment of brokenness became my breakthrough.

Fast forward two weeks, and I did make it to the leadership training. Right before I walked in the door, this wave washed over my body. I could feel that I was going to meet someone who was going to rock my world. I didn't know if it would be a male or a female, but I knew that whoever it was would change my life.

Sure enough, a guy who looked like Clark Kent with dark glasses sat down next to me. Our knees touched, and wow! It caught my attention.

A few seconds later, the facilitator of our four-month program gave us the ground rules. We were not allowed to have romantic relationships or do business with anyone in the course, among other things.

In that moment, I thought, "That's cool. I can go through this process and not be distracted by flirting with this guy next to me." Ironically, they asked us to pair up and have a buddy. He asked me if I wanted to be buddies, and I said yes.

The partnership was the most beautiful gift that was ever given to me. I now had a man in my life who would stand for me, no matter what. He challenged me in a beautiful way. We became best friends for the next four months. Then we started dating. A month later, we decided to get married!

I know I shocked a lot of friends and family when I got remarried after I'd just broken up with somebody.

My ex-husband and I still owned a business together. We had a phone call to work through details about shutting it down. We were still friends. At one point in the conversation, he asked if I was dating anybody. I said, "Yes I am, and I don't want to screw it up." Then I asked him, "Can you help me with any blind spots I might have in being a wife? Where did I not show up? Teach me how I can fix that, because I don't want to mess up this relationship. As a buddy, can you tell me where I screwed up?"

He was honest with me and said, "Stacey, I always felt like you had one foot out the door."

I had to agree with him. I spent so much time fantasizing about what life would be like without him that I never really stayed present. That didn't allow me to fully commit to him the way he deserved. I am grateful for him being very honest with me about how I could show up and play full out, so I could carry that forward into my next relationship.

When my current husband and I sat down and talked about the strong possibilities of being together, and what it means to be committed, we decided that both of us were going to play full out. We asked each other what it would look like if we both committed to that capacity. What kind of life, what possibilities could we build? How could we change lives together, as a team? My ex-husband's honestly made that conversation possible.

## My Tools & Rituals to Stay in the Flow

Quality time is one of my love languages. I'm a new stepmom, and I do my best to make quality time a priority. When it is our week to have the kids, we carve out quality time with them.

In my past relationship, we watched a lot of television. My new husband and I decided not to waste time with that. Conversations are more important to us, even with our kids. Screen time is limited. We eat dinner as a family and play a board game or a card game afterward. We enjoy listening to music together.

It's about carving quality time, because it goes by so quickly. That's where I find my peace and my playfulness. In the end, everybody's richer when your relationships are richer. That's my kind of prosperity—I value relationships. That's the kind of rich I want to be.

## My Purpose Is

My husband got inspired last year during our leadership training. He wanted to create an authentic piece of marketing that his clients, whom he coaches as a business consultant, could feel really good about putting out into the world. He was frustrated with Facebook ads, Google Ad Words, and other methods that rely on fear-based marketing.

He wondered, "What if we create a place where we could just share why people do what they do. Wouldn't that attract their ideal client?" So he decided to put it to the test. We created a venue, built a stage, and gave people three minutes to prove themselves and show humanity why they do what they do. In fact, you're not even allowed to talk about what you do, only why you do it. It's been a really beautiful process.

I think sometimes people float around life like zombies. They may have a passion for what they do, but they don't always know why they do it and where that inspiration came from. Once they tap into that, they can talk about their business on a whole new level. So instead of limiting it to a sentence on the About Page of their website, our process allows them to stand up, declare that why, and tell the world in an easy, three-minute format how that works for them.

We call it The Proof. It's two stages—a live stage in front of an audience of forty people where you declare your memorized monologue, and a virtual stage. Both are recorded. We give you those videos to use in your marketing. The first video is your why video from the live stage. For the second video, you get back on stage and sit with either myself or my husband. We interview you about what you do. We've found that the interview process is a great way to flesh out all the details that might otherwise be left out.

We're also considered a marketing agency, because we market for you on all of our platforms. You'll get your own profile page on our website, with beautiful black and white portraits of you, I use my expertise as a professional photographer to take them.

## My Gift for You

If you want to talk with us to see how we can turn your why into a really beautiful video, go to talktotheproof.com and click on the little red button to get on our calendar.

We'd love to talk to you in person and see if you're ready for the stage. We want to make sure that you're completely prepared to show up and declare your why. We'll help you do that.

Grab your gift from Stacey Lievens at: www.SuperwomanBook.com/gifts

## My Advice for You in Your Journey

Listen to your body, because it loves you and it talks to you all the time. You can tap in and listen to why you feel aches and pains, or why you feel tired or sick. Take it as an opportunity to slow down and have a conversation with it on a regular basis.

Listen to your body,
because it loves you and
it talks to you all the
time.

~ Stacey Lievens

# ABOUT THE AUTHOR

Maribel Jimenez is an International Speaker, Bestselling Author, Host of the Superwoman Entrepreneur Podcast and Marketing Launch Strategist.

She is the founder of Your Dream Launch and the Superwoman Entrepreneur communities where she teaches business and personal growth workshops to entrepreneurs, coaches, and consultants.

After pursuing her own dream of starting an online business so  she could be home with her kids, she turned around and began teaching others how they could do it too! Her passion is to help entrepreneurs tap into their brilliance, share it with the world and create a peaceful, playful, prosperous business—and life overall.

She's a happily married mom of four and loves having the freedom to spend time with her family and travel regularly. You can find out more about her free resources, group programs, retreats and consulting services at www.YourDreamLaunch.com.

# MEET THE SUPERWOMAN ENTREPRENEUR CO-AUTHORS

I invite you to meet all the Superwoman Entrepreneurs featured in this book and have free, unlimited access to thousands of dollars in personal development and business resources. All of this as our gift to support you on your SUPERwoman journey.

Plus, you can access behind-the-scenes video interviews with extra bonus resources!

**Access your Superwoman Entrepreneur Bonus Resources at: www.SuperwomanBook.com/gifts**

Behind every successful woman is a tribe of other successful women who have her back.